Defending Scilly

Defending Scilly

Mark Bowden and Allan Brodie

ENGLISH HERITAGE

Front cover
The incomplete Harry's Walls of the early 1550s overlook the harbour and St Mary's Pool. In the distance on the hilltop is Star Castle with the earliest parts of the Garrison Walls on the hillside below.
[DP085489]

Inside front cover
Woolpack Battery, the most heavily armed battery of the 1740s, commanded St Mary's Sound. Its strategic location led to the installation of a Defence Electric Light position in front of it in c 1900 and a pillbox was inserted into the tip of the battery during the Second World War.
[NMR 26571/007]

Frontispiece
From the late 16th century it was realised that a heavily fortified Garrison on St Mary's could guarantee control of the waters around the islands. In the 1740s new walls were built around large parts of it while in c 1900 6-in gun batteries surrounded by earthworks were set into the hillside.
[NMR 26571/001]

Acknowledgements
From this gun position on the platform beside Cromwell's Castle on Tresco any defenders could have fired on shipping trying to enter New Grimsby Harbour.
[DP025999]

Back cover
From the top of Cromwell's Castle Scilly's gunners could fire on any enemy ships that tried to moor in the harbour between Tresco and Bryher.
[DP085050]

Published by English Heritage, Kemble Drive, Swindon SN2 2GZ
www.english-heritage.org.uk
English Heritage is the Government's statutory adviser on all aspects of the historic environment.

© English Heritage 2011

Images (except as otherwise shown) © English Heritage.NMR

Maps on pages 95, 97 and the inside back cover are © Crown Copyright and database right 2011. All rights reserved. Ordnance Survey Licence number 100019088.

First published 2011

ISBN 978 1 84802 043 6

Product code 51530

British Library Cataloguing in Publication Data
A CIP catalogue record for this book is available from the British Library.

Application for the reproduction of images should be made to the National Monuments Record. Every effort has been made to trace the copyright holders and we apologise in advance for any unintentional omissions, which we would be pleased to correct in any subsequent edition of this book.

The National Monuments Record is the public archive of English Heritage. For more information, contact NMR Enquiry and Research Services, National Monuments Record Centre, Kemble Drive, Swindon SN2 2GZ; telephone (01793) 414600.

Typeset in ITC Charter 9.25pt on 13pt

Photographs by Mike Hesketh-Roberts
Aerial photographs by Damian Grady
Graphics by Deborah Cunliffe and Kate Parsons
Brought to publication by Jess Ward, Publishing, English Heritage
Edited by Susan Kelleher
Page layout by George Hammond
Printed in UK by Pureprint.

Contents

Acknowledgements

Martin Fletcher was the first person to involve us with research about Scilly during the preparation of a draft management plan for the Garrison Walls in 2006. Alongside his work excavations were conducted on some of the surviving earthworks. A report on these was completed by Dave Fellows and is available in the National Monuments Record in Swindon.

During the current project, which began in 2008, Mike Hesketh-Roberts has been a key member, taking hundreds of photographs unrivalled in their quality and he has supervised their use in this publication until his retirement. Damian Grady took the superb aerial photographs that have been used in this book, revealing archaeological sites in unprecedented clarity. Deborah Cunliffe has prepared the excellent archaeological survey drawings for publication and Kate Parsons, with advice from Nigel Fradgley, has produced beautiful maps to help readers to find the most significant military monuments. David Andrews has kindly provided the drawing of the Garrison Gate from rectified photographs. Roger JC Thomas has used his considerable expertise on military archaeology to fine tune this book and Barry Jones has provided invaluable comments on the evolving manuscript. We would also like to thank Phil McMahon, Simon Ramsden and Heather Sebire, for their insights throughout the project and thanks also to Peter Murphy for his useful advice and information. In the Publications Department we would like to thank Jess Ward for bringing the manuscript to publication.

Paul Pattison and his colleagues Susan Greaney and Sarah Tatham undertook the new interpretation of English Heritage properties alongside this research project and they have kindly allowed us to use some of the artwork that Mark Fenton and Phil Kenning of Kenning Illustration & Creative Design Limited have prepared for this. Paul has also read the manuscript and from the outset made his vast knowledge of all matters military available to the project team.

A huge amount of research lies behind this book, and thanks must go to the staff of the National Archives, the British Library and the Cornwall Record Office for their assistance. Most of this research cannot find its way into this publication, but will be used in more detailed articles that will be published subsequently.

This book has relied heavily on the warmth and hospitality of everyone we have met during our visits to Scilly. A key point of contact has been the Council of the Isles of Scilly where the Conservation Officer Eleanor Breen and the officer of the Isles of Scilly Area of Outstanding Natural Beauty (AONB) Dr Trevor Kirk have provided us with material and emotional assistance. Their boss Craig Dryden has generously allowed us to draw on the considerable expertise in his team. We would also like to thank the two land stewards of the Duchy of Cornwall Colin Sturmer and his successor Chris Gregory who have been informative and welcoming to us on our various visits. We have also been made welcome by the owners and staff of the Star Castle, and Ted and Barbara Moulson have kindly given us access to their holiday site and the former barracks of *c* 1900 that now serves as holiday accommodation.

A particular tribute is owed to David Mawer and his hardworking team of staff and volunteers from the Isles of Scilly Wildlife Trust. Their grazing programme is attempting to reinstate the natural balance of the islands' coastline through selective grazing, and therefore they have begun to reveal more of the islands' military heritage, and undoubtedly more remains to be found.

We have also relied greatly on local expertise to make contacts, locate sites and identify research. Richard McCarthy has shared his research on the civil wars and kindly read and commented on the manuscript. Katherine Sawyer has generously shared her time and Richard Larn's work on shipwrecks has highlighted the naval significance of Scilly. Unfortunately this book could not address this rich vein of Scilly's military heritage, but ongoing research is continuing to reveal more of this important legacy.

A final and a very special accolade must be reserved for Amanda Martin, the curator of the Isles of Scilly Museum. Unknown to her she has become the unofficial research assistant for the project, providing quick replies to all the questions that we had forgotten to ask when we had been on the islands. The museum contains an unrivalled collection of material about Scilly in general and its defences in particular, and she has kindly allowed us to use all of the research material in her care, some of it being published for the first time.

Foreword

The Isles of Scilly, covered with wild flowers and bathed in warm sunshine, attract visitors to marvel at the natural beauty and enjoy their tranquillity. However, these idyllic islands have also been in the frontline of England's and later Britain's defences since the 16th century. Structures from each of the phases of conflict over the past 450 years have survived, ranging from small 16th-century forts on Tresco to the string of Second World War pillboxes defending St Mary's.

Scilly's military heritage is unmatched anywhere else in Britain in terms of its layers of evidence, but it is a heritage under threat, not from marauding Spanish ships or German dive bombers, but from the power of the sea. Coastal military defences are inevitably vulnerable, and erosion seems to have already claimed some of the earthworks recorded on the islands. Growing concerns about climate change, with increasingly tempestuous weather patterns and rising sea level, means that this process may be accelerating and parts of Scilly's largest settlement, Hugh Town, lying on a former sandbank just above sea level could be in danger.

This book describes the colourful military history of Scilly, but it also seeks to illustrate the value and fragility of our coastal heritage in general. Government and local authorities face difficult decisions about protecting the coastline, and cost inevitably means that only parts of the coastline can be hardened against the sea. Whatever the future for our coastline, a vital first stage is to document and enjoy its precious heritage.

Baroness Andrews, Chair of English Heritage

Glossary

Bastion – a gun platform projecting from a defensive work, usually with two 'flanks' and two 'faces'. Guns in the flanks fired to protect the wall and adjacent bastions from close attack; guns on the faces fired at a more distant enemy. Each bastion was a precise angular shape so that its guns covered a certain area of ground. Guns on adjacent bastions covered the same area of ground so that deadly crossfires were set up.

Bivouac platforms – small terraced areas where the soldiers pitched their tents, or perhaps had wooden huts.

Breastwork – a temporary field fortification built a few feet high to form a protected firing position for infantry or guns.

Carronade – a short smoothbore artillery piece in use from the 1770s. It was a short-range weapon used aboard ship and in fortifications, firing a heavy ball or scattering a lethal shower of shot.

Casemate – a vaulted chamber built into the thickness of the ramparts of a fortress and used for various purposes including accommodation, storage and for defence.

Culverin – a heavy artillery piece, with a calibre of about 5 to 5½ins (127–140mm), which fired a shot of about 15lbs (6.8kg) to a maximum range of 2,000yds (1.8km).

Demi-culverin – a medium artillery piece, with a calibre of about 4½ins (114mm), which fired a shot of about 9lbs (4kg) to a maximum range of 1,600yds (1.4km).

Embrasure – an opening in a defensive wall, usually with splayed sides, through which an artillery piece fired.

The **Garrison** – one of a pair of land masses (effectively separate islands) making up St Mary's linked by a sandbar on which Hugh Town was established.

Imprest – a sum of money paid in advance to cover future works, and vacated or reconciled (ie accounted for) when bills or receipts are submitted later.

Minion – a light artillery piece with a calibre of about 3ins (76mm), which fired a shot of about 4lbs (1.8kg) to a maximum range of 1,400yds (1.2km).

Orillon – literally the 'ear' of a bastion, an extension (usually rounded) to the inside of a bastion face that served to hide and protect artillery pieces positioned in the retired flank.

Redan – a V-shaped projection from a fortification enabling defenders to make limited flanking and crossfires against attackers.

Redoubt – a small but strongly defended enclosed fortification, sometimes positioned outside a larger fortress or on a dominant topographical feature. It could provide cover for a vulnerable or strategically important position.

Saker – a light artillery piece with a calibre of about 3½ins (89mm), which fired a shot of about 5lbs (2.3kg) to a maximum range of 1,500yds (1.4km).

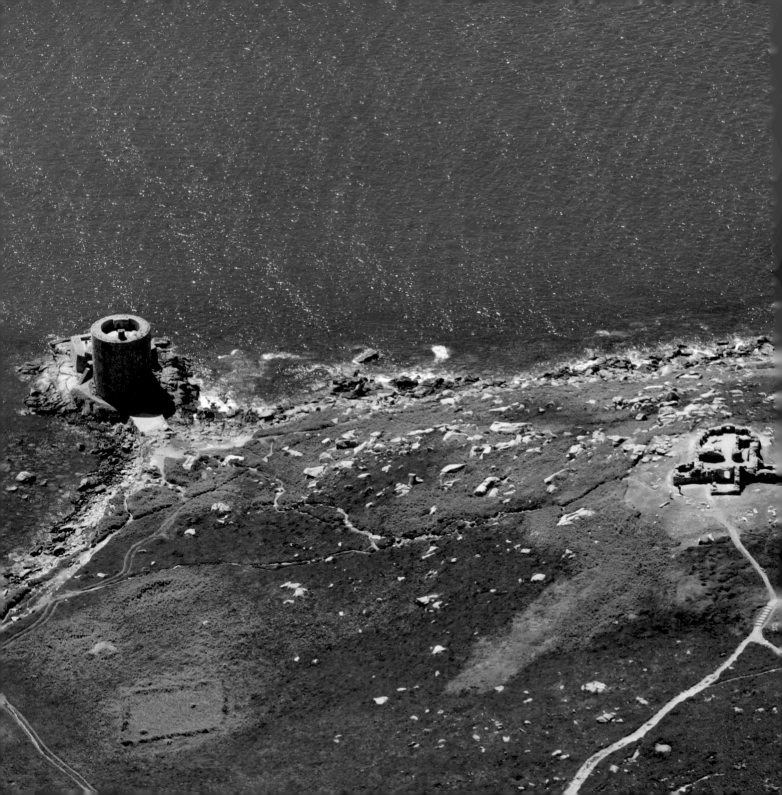

1

Introduction

'Two causes of the extinction of the old Inhabitants, their habitations, and works of Peace, War, and Religion, occur to me; the gradual advances of the Sea, and a sudden submersion of the Land.'[1]

In the middle of the 18th century the Cornish antiquary, geologist and naturalist William Borlase recognised and recorded some of Scilly's rich military legacy that had endured against the power of the sea. From the mid-16th century onwards national government had realised the strategic significance of the Isles of Scilly, and in 1602 Sir Francis Godolphin stated that: 'no other place can so aptly permit or restrain the traffic of Ireland and the north of Scotland with France or Spain.'[2] He was lobbying for further funds to improve the islands' defences, which by this date consisted of two forts on Tresco built during Edward VI's reign (1547–53), as well as the incomplete Harry's Walls of the early 1550s and the Elizabethan Star Castle on the Garrison (1593). By the early 17th century the first stretch of the Garrison Walls had been built running from near the harbour to the two Benham Batteries.

These structures were built to protect Scilly and its safe anchorages from the French or Spanish, who fortunately never came, but when shots were fired in anger it was between Englishmen. During the civil wars St Mary's was provided with an extensive network of earthwork batteries and breastworks, some of which survive today.

By the 1740s these defences were felt to be inadequate and in some places were falling into the sea. Therefore, between 1741 and 1746 new, substantial batteries with a mile of interconnecting walls were built around the east and south side of the Garrison (Fig 1). Again huge expenditure was invested in defences, but the enemy, in this case the French, never came.

During the wars with France from 1793 to 1815 the Garrison Walls were rearmed, but no new major fortifications were built, the Navy being seen as the first and main line of defence. After 1815 Scilly's defences were neglected and in 1863 the garrison manning the walls was disbanded.

A generation later a perceived new threat from France led to the creation of a series of gun batteries supplemented by large searchlights to combat the rapidly developing French navy. However, with the signing of the *Entente Cordiale* in 1904 the danger from France disappeared and the batteries that had received their guns were disarmed.

In the late 1540s King Charles' Castle was built on the hill overlooking New Grimsby Harbour and an earthwork was placed around it, probably in 1627. The tall cylindrical tower of Cromwell's Castle replaced or supplemented a Tudor blockhouse by the early 1650s.
[NMR 23934/002]

1

Scilly was an ideal base for shipping, but with the advent of aerial warfare it also proved to be a strategic location for aircraft to patrol the sea lanes around the west of England. During the First World War a large seaplane base was established at New Grimsby on Tresco, while in the Second World War the recently opened civil airport became home to a flight of RAF Hurricanes.

During the Second World War Scilly was attacked and its aircraft managed on some occasions to sight or engage the enemy, but as for most of the previous four centuries the threat of attack from foreign enemies was never realised. This has left Scilly with a unique military legacy that provides a cross-section through the threats that Britain has faced.

There have been some losses, not due to later development but as a result

Figure 1
This stretch of the Garrison Walls, with Colonel George Boscawen's Battery in the distance, was being built between 1744 and 1746. It helps to illustrate the scale of the project taking place during that decade, a task that ended abruptly a short distance to the west of this battery.
[DP022498]

of the action of the sea (Fig 2). Thousands of years ago the receding ice age began the rise in sea level that ultimately created the cluster of islands that we know as the Isles of Scilly. More recently, in the 18th century, William Borlase recognised the impact of an ever-changing coastline and advancing sea that had engulfed 'works of Peace, War and Religion'. Today Scilly's extensive coastline is even more vulnerable as climate change brings an increased threat of turbulent storms while the rising sea level will make low-lying settlements such as Hugh Town on St Mary's more prone to flooding.

Climate change is forcing the Government to make difficult choices and while its priorities inevitably mean that most funding will be concentrated on assets of high economic value, there is a need to highlight the wealth of our coastal heritage and its vulnerability. Although this book concentrates on Scilly's military defences, hopefully it will serve to illustrate the value of England's wider coastal heritage to an island nation, and while we may not be able to protect it all, we can rightly celebrate it and debate its future.

Figure 2
Once part of the circuit of Second World War defences,
the pillbox at Pendrathen has succumbed to the rapid
erosion of the coastline and now sits on the rocks.
[DP085375]

2

Scilly's military heritage

Before the 16th century Scilly's major fortification was Ennor Castle, overlooking Old Town Bay on St Mary's, which is first mentioned in the 13th century. The antiquarian John Leland tersely described it in the 1530s as 'a meately strong pile', while in 1756 William Borlase noted that 'part of the walls still remains'.[3] Today all that can be seen is a small wooded mound and none of the walls mentioned by Borlase remain visible above ground. Another enigmatic site, which could be 16th century or earlier, is to be found at the southern end of the Garrison near the *c* 1900 Woolpack Battery. This is marked on Christian Lilly's map of 1715 as 'The Folly or Old Barracks' and depicted as a diamond-orientated square structure with large corner buttresses. Among some earthworks and features dating from 20th-century conflicts a similarly orientated structure has survived as a shallow earthwork, its shallowness suggesting considerable antiquity compared to the clarity of the newer defences (*see* Figs 22, 38 and 83).

By the reign of Henry VIII the need for national initiatives had been recognised by the Crown. In 1538 England faced invasion by the combined forces of the Emperor Charles V and the King of France Francis I who were seeking to reestablish papal authority. This threat prompted the construction of a series of fortifications along the coast of England and Wales, stretching from Hull round to Milford Haven.

The defences of Edward VI and Mary I 1547–58

Fortifying Scilly was not part of the Henrician programme, but some elements of it were reflected in the structures built on Tresco and St Mary's during the short reign of Edward VI. He was only nine years old when he became king and therefore a ruling council was established, though it quickly became dominated by its leader Edward Seymour, 1st Duke of Somerset. He was the Lord Protector of England between the death of Henry VIII in 1547 and his fall from power in 1549. His younger brother, Thomas, was the Lord Admiral and in April 1547 he visited Scilly. Within a year the Crown had begun to commit some money towards Scilly's defences, and in the following year £362 was sent to pay for soldiers who were manning and perhaps building fortifications.

Although Scilly might be remote from London and central government, its defences were often up-to-date in design and the incomplete Harry's Walls is one of the earliest examples of angled bastions anywhere in England. [NMR 26572/023]

With the fall of the Lord Protector in October 1549 an examination of the progress of the defences in Scilly was ordered. Captain William Tyrrell was sent to examine all aspects of the defences. The most important part of his brief was that: 'He must consider whether the forts are best placed for defence, their strength and, if they are not completed, the charges of finishing them; what store there is, and order further provision as requisite. If the forts are not best placed and are not mostly completed he may order their stay until further order.'[4]

Tresco

In the first years of Edward VI's reign building work on the islands seems to have focussed on Tresco. The likely order of construction is that the buildings there, King Charles' Castle and the Old Blockhouse, were built from 1548 onwards, with work on Harry's Walls on St Mary's only beginning in 1551. King Charles' Castle and the Old Blockhouse belong to an earlier tradition of fortification design compared to Harry's Walls. There was also a Tudor blockhouse where Cromwell's Castle now stands and the form of its circular tower is suspiciously similar in type to the core block of the large Henrician castles. However, a document of 1554 describes a much more modest structure with just two guns and two chambers. These structures were built to command the two stretches of Tresco where enemy forces could be landed. The Old Blockhouse overlooked Old Grimsby Harbour on the east side, while King Charles' Castle overlooked the northern entrance to New Grimsby Harbour on the west. Any structure on the site of Cromwell's Castle would have attacked ships that managed to evade fire from King Charles' Castle.

The Old Blockhouse is the smaller of the two mid-16th century fortifications on Tresco (Figs 3 and 4). It consists of a paved square platform that could have accommodated three guns and the walls around it have been reduced in height (Fig 5). There is no evidence of how or whether the platform was roofed. On the south side there is a built-in locker, presumably for powder, and attached to the west side there is a small room lit by two windows and heated by a fireplace. This room blocks a window opening in the west wall of the platform, but there is no obvious joint in the south wall indicating that the two parts of the structure were from different dates. Around the building there is a shallow bank that could be contemporary or may date from the Civil War.

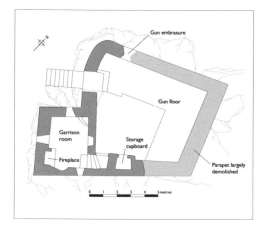

Figure 3 (above)
The Old Blockhouse consisted of a small platform with an attached room with a small fireplace, the modest accommodation for those manning the fortification. This room blocks a window of the gun platform, suggesting that it may have been an addition.

Figure 4 (above, right)
Overlooking Old Grimsby Harbour, the Old Blockhouse of the late 1540s was surrounded by a small earthwork, perhaps of the same date. This fort was at the heart of the battle for Tresco in 1651.
[DP085145]

Figure 5 (right)
Inside the Old Blockhouse by the side entrance to the gun platform is the remains of one embrasure marking a firing position and a strange, flat stone providing some covering beside the door.
[DP085137]

On the other side of Tresco a much more ambitious structure was erected (Fig 6). King Charles' Castle consists of a canted, polygonal gun room or platform originally with five gun embrasures, though one was abandoned later when a small room was created in the north-east corner (Figs 7 and 8). Attached to the east side of it there is a large room, the northern half of which was used as a kitchen for the soldiers manning the castle (Fig 9). Attached to the north and south ends of this room are small, square bedchambers. Although unheated, the northern room has a triangular, stone floor in one corner, perhaps for a small brazier. A large porch or guardroom protects the entrance to the building. There is some architectural stonework lying around the outside of the building though whether there is sufficient to recreate a full upper storey is unclear.

Figure 6
Sitting on Castle Down on Tresco, King Charles' Castle has commanding views of the entrance to New Grimsby Harbour. Briefly involved in the fighting during the Civil War, it was used as soldiers' lodgings in the 1660s.
[NMR 23933/028]

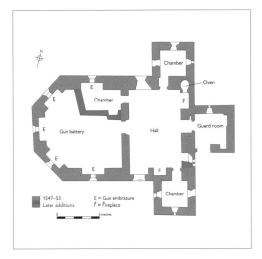

Figure 7 (above)
King Charles' Castle consisted of a polygonal gun battery for five guns with an attached block of domestic accommodation. This consisted of a large room serving as a hall and kitchen, with two small chambers, presumably bedrooms.

Figure 8 (above, right)
Here are two of the firing positions for artillery pieces in the gun room of King Charles' Castle, designed to prevent shipping entering the harbour below. There is no evidence of how it was covered over and whether there was an upper storey to the building.
[DP085116]

Figure 9 (right)
The landward side of King Charles' Castle was equipped with service accommodation comprising a main room with a large fireplace and a bread oven, while the pointed-arched door to the left led into one of the chambers. The main entrance to the right of the fireplace contains a bemused archaeologist.
[DP085108]

The Tresco buildings date from the early part of the reign of Edward VI but their form was derived from some of the buildings erected late in Henry VIII's reign. King Charles' Castle resembles in general terms Sandsfoot Castle (1540) at Weymouth, a former castle on Brownsea Island (1543) and some of the blockhouses built in 1539–40 on the Thames, such as at West Tilbury and Gravesend. In all these fortifications, small blocks provided domestic accommodation alongside a polygonal gun platform.

The Old Blockhouse had a slight earthwork bank around it. In providing an earthwork to accompany a blockhouse the builders may have been following a practice that had been used in the construction of at least one of the Thames blockhouses at West Tilbury, which was set within a small enclosure. King Charles' Castle is located at the south-west corner of a larger, more ambitious earthwork (Fig 10). It is roughly square in plan with a bastion at its north-west corner and a demi-bastion at its north-east corner. On 28 May 1627 Bernard Johnson 'engenier to his Majestie' was instructed that 'he shall have occasion to cut turffe and earth, take timber, carts and other caryages, and lykewise to hire workmen' for work at Pendennis and in Scilly.[5] This seems to be the most likely date for the earthwork around King Charles' Castle. A similar earthwork was, coincidentally, added around Sandsfoot Castle in the 1620s and there were comparable new defences at Pendennis and were at least intended at St Mawes, Cornwall.

A couple of hundred metres to the south-east of King Charles' Castle there is another 400m long earthwork across the plateau (Fig 11). It has a central bastion with orillons with a half bastion further east and possibly a fragment of another to the west. This is a very slight earthwork and must be regarded as a laying-out preparation rather than a fully fledged defensive work. It may belong to the 1550s when orillons first began to appear in military architecture in England, including being used in Harry's Walls on St Mary's.

St Mary's

The first definite reference to work on Harry's Walls on St Mary's occurs on 27 May 1551: 'A letter to John Kelligrewe to make the forte in our Ladies Isle at Silley upon the little hill betwixt the freshe water and St. Marie Roode, whereof to receave a plat at his sonnes handes; and to cover the one half

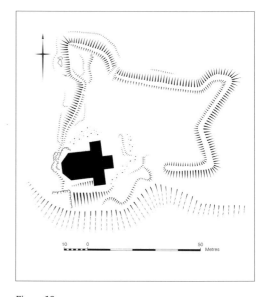

Figure 10
Around King Charles' Castle an earthwork, now seemingly incomplete, was created, perhaps in 1627. Unlike earthworks created under pressure during the Civil War this has an unhurried, almost textbook appearance.

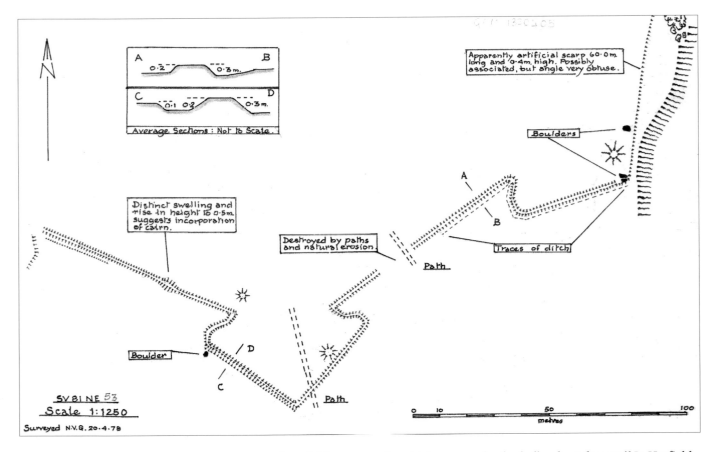

A   B
0·2   0·3 m.

C   D
0·1 0·2   0·3 m.

Average Sections : Not to Scale.

Apparently artificial scarp 60·0m. long and 0·4m. high. Possibly associated, but angle very obtuse.

Boulders

Distinct swelling and rise in height to 0·5m. suggests incorporation of cairn.

Destroyed by paths and natural erosion.

A

B

Traces of ditch

Path

Boulder

D

C

Path

SV 81 NE 53
Scale 1:1250

Surveyed N.V.Q. 20·4·78

0   10   50   100
metres

Figure 11
This survey card, created by Norman Quinnell in the 1970s, was the basis for the information about the earthworks on Castle Down used on modern Ordnance Survey maps.

therof this sommer, for which purpose leade shalbe shortely sent.'[6] In Hatfield House, Hertfordshire, there is a plan of Harry's Walls, which bears the legend:

This fortress begonne in our ladies Ilande for the defence of the whole Isles, and not finished, the tymberworke for the same alredy framid to the setting up, with a brewhouse & a milne lying in South Wales, redy to be conveyed to the saide Isles, when order may be given as touching the same.[7]

This has sometimes been thought to be the Killigrew plan of the fort, but it cannot be the design drawing as its legend says it is a plan of a building that had already been begun (Fig 12).

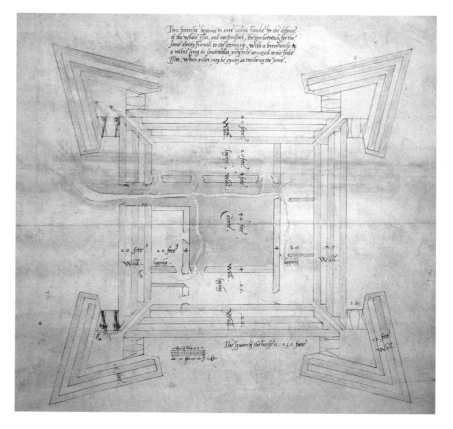

This fortresse begonne in oure ladies Iaunde for the defence
of the whole Isles, and not finished, the tymber worke for the
same alredy framed to the setting up, with a brewhouse &
a milne lying in sowerwalles, redy to be conveyed to the saide
Isles, when order may be given as touching the same.

The guard of the house is. 150. foote.

Figure 12
This plan seems to date from the early 1550s and shows how Harry's Walls would have been constructed. The caption suggests that within the thick stone walls there would have been lodgings for its garrison.
[CPM/1/58 Reproduction courtesy of The Marquess of Salisbury]

Harry's Walls was never completed. All that remains today is the western side of the lower parts of the fort with two acutely pointed bastions linked by a stretch of curtain wall, while the ditch for the north side has been cut through the rocky ground (Figs 13 and 14 and *see page 4*).

The form of the bastions allowed flanking fire, as is indicated by the pairs of guns in the Hatfield House plan, and this reflected the latest thinking in military engineering in England. These ideas imported from Italy seem to have first appeared in England at Portsmouth in 1546 and at Yarmouth Castle in *c* 1547. Angled bastions were also the basis of the new fort, the Citadel and the slightly later town defences being erected in distant Berwick-upon-Tweed roughly contemporary with the construction of Harry's Walls.

Figure 13 (right, above)
This plan of Harry's Walls shows that only two of the angled bastions and one interconnecting stretch of wall were completed. Inside the footprint of the proposed fort there are features in the ground suggesting some man-made structures, though it is difficult to reconcile them with the 1550s plan.

Figure 14 (right, below)
This view of Harry's Walls, from the southern to the northern bastion, shows how bastions of this shape allowed covering fire along the face of the fortification. In 1554 the incomplete fort was said to be armed with two sakers: small-calibre pieces of artillery.
[DP085488]

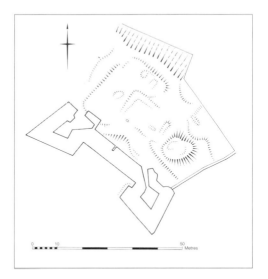

In September 1551 John Killigrew junior was asked to provide the 'Receyvour of the countie of Cornewall' with the accounts of how the money had been spent.[8] When the books were submitted they revealed that between 1548 and 1552 £3,123 18s 9d had been spent on the defences of Tresco and St Mary's. Thereafter, there is no definite reference to the main building campaign until the 1590s and the principal victim of this sudden cessation of work was Harry's Walls. The reason for it not being completed has variously been ascribed to it being on the wrong site and on a site that was too small. Instead the reason for its incompletion is that the Crown ran out of money. In September 1552 a document collated all the expenditure on the military that had taken place in the previous decade. On fortifications alone, Henry VIII had spent a staggering £181,179 12s 6⅞d, while in the five years of his youthful successor a further £35,228 18s 2¼d had been spent. When wages were added, the decade had seen a total of £290,662 16s 6⅛d being spent on England's defences. Scilly accounted for a paltry £3,787 6s 2½d spent on

buildings while a further £4,184 7s 1d was expended on wages. However, such levels of expenditure nationally could not be sustained. Scilly was just another victim of the wider economic environment and for the next 40 years there would be no new construction on the islands.

The defences of Scilly 1558–1640

Queen Elizabeth's decision in 1585 to provide the Netherlands with support in its struggle for independence from Spain triggered almost two decades of undeclared war. In August 1587 a fleet of 120 Spanish ships was reported off Scilly and in the following year the Spanish Armada failed to instigate the invasion of England. However, the Spanish continued to be a particular threat to Scilly, particularly after 1590 when they seized and held a foothold in Brittany for a short time.

In response, by March 1591/2 a plan had been 'drawne for the fortefienge of the Iles of Sylley and especiallie St. Marie Iland, for defence of the roade'.[9] The same meeting of the Privy Council that accepted the plan also instructed Robert Adams 'a man of verie good skill and knowledge' to go to Scilly to examine the works that had already taken place and to establish how to complete them according to the original plan or in a better fashion. It seems from the accompanying documents that consideration was being given to completing Harry's Walls, but Adams was briefed to consider other options to protect St Mary's.

By May 1593 the plan for the defences had been finalised. On 14 May 1593 Robert Adams was given written authority to start the project and on 6 August 1593 Sir Francis Godolphin, Governor of the Isles of Scilly, wrote to Lord Burghley enthusing about the progress that had been made. In December 1594, when Star Castle was completed, the cost had reached £958 11s 2d, of which only £450 had been paid.

Star Castle is a small eight-pointed, star-shaped fort set within similarly shaped outer defences surrounded by a deep, dry ditch (Figs 15, 16 and 17). Its form can be said to be an updated version of a large 1540s Henrician fort with pointed angles rather than rounded bastions. The central building, which is two

Figure 15
Commanding the north end of the Garrison, and therefore overlooking the Road between St Mary's and Tresco, Star Castle almost appears as if it has come from a textbook of a Renaissance military engineer. Small buildings in the four corners of the castle were barracks for soldiers and were repaired after 1715.
[NMR 26576/036]

storied with an attic and a small basement, contained the domestic accommodation of the castle. Around the building there is a narrow passage and a series of outbuildings, including stores. These serve as the base for the rampart around the perimeter of the castle on which there were to be eight pieces of artillery. Joints in the walls of the parapet indicate the location of these gun positions, while loops in the parapet provided firing positions for muskets. Star Castle is entered from the north through a square-headed, moulded door with the date of 1593 on its lintel (Fig 18). This door gave access to a passage protected by a gun position and a portcullis that was added in *c* 1600.

Sir Francis Godolphin and Robert Adams may have originally thought they were providing a formidable military structure, at least for the money that was available, but as early as 6 August 1593 Godolphin had already identified that Star Castle on its own would be inadequate to defend St Mary's:

> When the fort and house are ended, many works should be speedily performed, as three blockhouses, four platforms, all the ordnance carriages newly made, and a trench and bank to compass the hill near the sea, to shadow the men from discovery by the shipping.[10]

Four platforms would describe the stretch of the Garrison Walls running from north to south from Well Battery to the two Benham Batteries and this is where the walling with the earliest character is found (Fig 19). The purpose of

Figure 16 (above, left)
The imposing main façade of Star Castle shows the heavily fortified gate and the parapets with musket-loops and originally with gaps for eight pieces of artillery. The bell above the entrance was a warning bell of any imminent attack.
[DP085292]

Figure 17 (above)
As well as thick walls and formidable firepower, Star Castle boasted a dry moat around it for further protection. In the Road a cruise ship is disgorging passengers for a fleeting visit to St Mary's.
[DP085295]

Figure 18 (right)
The entrance to Star Castle bears the date 1593 and the initials of Queen Elizabeth I, Sir Francis Godolphin and Robert Adams, the last two being set at the base of the door jambs. To fend off unwelcome intruders a gun position is set inside the door.
[DP022350]

Figure 19 (right)
The earliest stage of the Garrison Walls, dating from the 1590s, is easily recognised by large irregular stones with small packing pieces used to the joints. At the far right of this photograph is more regular stonework where the rebuilt Garrison Gate of 1742 was inserted into the original walls.
[DP022358]

these walls was to protect the flank of Star Castle from attack by any forces that may have been landed on the beaches below.

The continuing strategic significance of Scilly was such that in 1600 Godolphin prepared a four-page letter petitioning for improved defences for the islands. He wanted to provide Star Castle with a stronger parapet, and to fill in the rampart by creating three casemates as well as adding the portcullis at the gate. For the protection of the islands, Godolphin requested £200 to create three new blockhouses on Nut Rock to protect 'St Mary Sound or Road', at 'Portlistry' to cover Crow Sound and on Tresco on 'dobrock' to protect the harbour at New Grimsby.[11] Each of these was to be large enough for at least three or four pieces of ordnance – with the top paved in stone to support the ordnance – and 15ft-high walls, 10ft of which was to be filled with earth.

There are several problems with this list of sites. Nut Rock is an unsuitable place for a blockhouse, but in the Parliamentary Survey of 1651 Rat Island is said to have had a blockhouse – a location not mentioned in Godolphin's letter. The second blockhouse was to be at 'Portlistry', presumably somewhere near Pelistry Bay. Today there are remains of a small, rectangular structure at Block

House Point and a 1554 survey of the ordnance on the islands contains a reference to a blockhouse in this area. In the late 17th century and the mid-18th century the blockhouse still featured on charts as a navigational feature. On Tresco the new blockhouse mentioned in 1600 was to protect the harbour at New Grimsby, much as Cromwell's Castle does today. However, in 1554 there already seems to have been a blockhouse on this site. Was Godolphin seeking funds in 1600 to replace a modest existing structure? Within the early 1650s tower of Cromwell's Castle there is a datestone on the inside face of the door on to the gun platform which has the incised legend 'M1591H'. However, this is probably a reset stone as its inconspicuous location is at odds with its commemorative contents.

In the early 17th century changes on the international political scene allowed Scilly a brief respite from preparations for conflict. After Philip II of Spain's death in 1598 and Elizabeth I's death in 1603 England and Spain were able to conclude a peace treaty. However, with the outbreak of war with Spain again in 1624, the accession of Charles I in 1625 and renewed warfare with France, there was a reassessment of the state of the defences. On 3 April 1627 a warrant for £800 was issued to repair 'the Fort of St. Mary's', while in May of the same year the order was issued apparently to construct earthworks around King Charles' Castle on Tresco.[12] David Portius and Nicholas Geevelo from Holland were in the Isles of Scilly in December 1627 to help with improving the fortifications. It is not clear what works they performed, but the 'Fort', less than 40 years old, was still said to be inadequate in 1631. Although there had been calls for more investment in the fortifications, little had happened as in 1637 yet another assessment was being prepared: 'The Castle is unable to lodge a garrison of 20 men, and incapable of defence.'[13]

The death of Sir Francis Godolphin in 1639–40, the grandson of the builder of Star Castle, seems to have ended this particular process of seeking money for improvements, with little having been achieved. Perhaps the only major building dating from this period may be the magazine near the Garrison Gate, which seems to be an early 17th-century structure with 18th-century alterations (Figs 20 and 21). There are no references to its construction, but it does appear on a 1655 map in the Cornwall Record Office (*see* Fig 22). Although there were still threats from abroad, the next hostilities in Scilly would come not from France or Spain, but from within Britain.

Figure 20
Probably dating from the 1620s, though with considerable later alterations and reconstructions, the magazine near the entrance to the Garrison has a strong vaulted ceiling and very thick walls. These are only pierced by small openings to provide some ventilation and to admit a little light from lamps or candles kept safely outside the structure.
[DP085223]

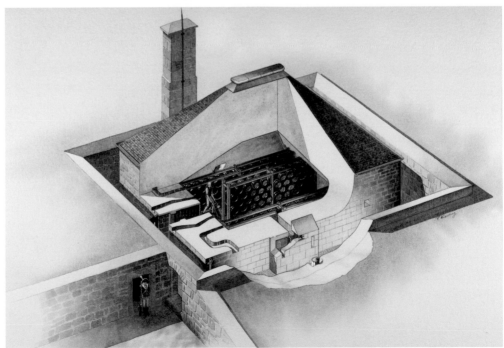

Figure 21
The magazine was set within a walled enclosure built into the hillside – measures designed to prevent explosions damaging Star Castle and the Garrison Walls. What appears to be a chimney was a structure onto which a vital lightning conductor was attached.

The Wars of the Three Kingdoms

Scilly has always been strategically significant and during the civil wars of the mid-17th century (1642–51) its location between Britain and France, and between Britain and Ireland was paramount – particularly when one side in the conflict, the Royalists, was dependent on privateering for their survival. The Parliamentarian assault on the islands in April 1651 was the only recorded occasion, until the 20th century, when the islands actually experienced military conflict.

For much of the early part of the war (1642–6) the Isles of Scilly were held for the Royalists under their Governor, Sir Francis Godolphin, and already privateers were operating from the islands. During the spring of 1646 Charles, Prince of Wales was a refugee in the islands following the defeat of the Royalist forces in south-west England at the Battle of Torrington and their final surrender at Tresillian Bridge on 15 March 1646. After his departure for Jersey, and subsequently the Continent, Parliament's naval forces began to blockade the islands and forced the surrender of the garrison. Parliament held the islands until September 1648 when the garrison rebelled against the Governor, Colonel Anthony Buller, and declared for the king. The young and combative Sir John Grenville arrived shortly after from Jersey and under his command Scilly became a major privateering base preying on British and Dutch vessels. Scilly was also, potentially, a stepping stone and base for Royalist Irish troops mounting an invasion of England.

Parliament's attempts to counter the privateers were largely ineffective, but by the end of 1650 the Dutch authorities had decided to react to the attacks on their shipping. In March 1651 a squadron under Maarten Tromp was sent to obtain the release of ships and their crews, and to extract reparations from Grenville. The English Parliament feared a Dutch attempt to capture and hold the islands, and so immediately fitted out an expedition under Robert Blake, General-at-Sea, to retake them. After an initial assault was repulsed, Blake took Tresco and Bryher on 18–20 April. By 5 May Blake's guns were bombarding St Mary's Pool and the Road, and shortly afterwards the Royalists were forced to surrender.

Many of the earthwork batteries and breastworks that survive on the islands have been attributed to this period and most historians incline to the

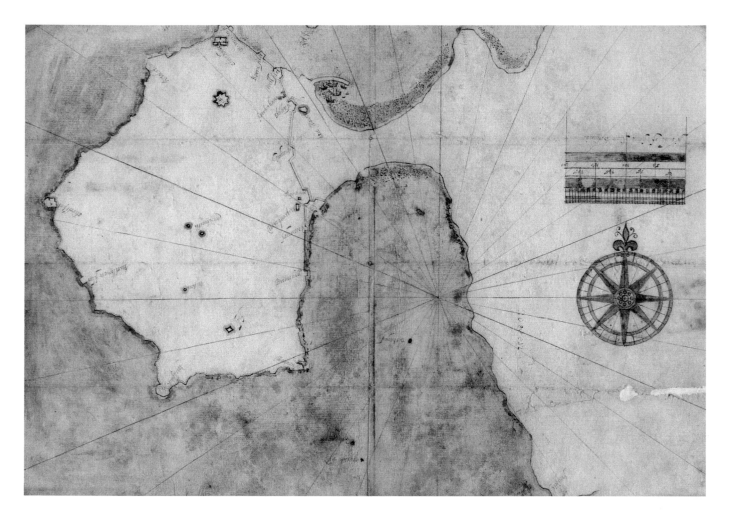

Figure 22
This map of 1655 includes the earliest survey of the Garrison. It shows Star Castle near the top with the Storehouse above, and to the right can be seen the earliest part of the Garrison Walls. Elsewhere the coastline was defended by earthworks, shown as a line of dots with some more substantial batteries along the circuit.
[Courtesy of the Cornwall Record Office GO/575]

view that nearly all of them were built by the Royalist Governor Grenville between 1649 and 1651 (Fig 22). The exceptions are Oliver's Battery on Carn Near, Tresco, which is known to have been built by Blake's forces in April–May 1651, and a battery on Peninnis, the construction of which, it has been claimed, is recorded in the early 18th century. However, there are significant differences in style and scale amongst the earthworks and it is probable that the origins of these works were more varied.

The earthworks around King Charles' Castle on Tresco may belong to the 1620s, while the nearby linear earthwork on Castle Down may belong to the mid-16th century (*see* Figs 10 and 11). What part they played, if any, in the Royalist commander William Edgecumbe's brief defence of the castle on

Figure 23
Along the west side of the Garrison the proposed walls of the 1740s were never built, meaning that a long stretch of the breastworks and some earthwork batteries have survived. These are on the edge of the cliff and are in danger of falling into the sea.
[DP022630]

19–20 April 1651 is not known, but the effort in providing extensive defences on St Mary's suggests that the Royalists thought, erroneously, that the defence of that island was the key to retaining control of Scilly.

There are records of a large number of earthwork batteries on St Mary's, many of them connected by breastworks, as well as a redoubt on the Gugh and batteries on Samson and Bryher. Recent fieldwork has failed to confirm the existence of all of these sites; some are undoubtedly concealed by the dense vegetation that smothers parts of the coastline following the decline of traditional grazing, but some may already have been lost to the sea (Fig 23).

Of the batteries and related sites examined, some fall into distinct types while others appear to be unique. The most common type of battery is a V-shaped earthwork, usually sited on the coast above low cliffs; all the earthwork batteries on the Garrison are of this type and other examples can be seen at Morval Point, Church Point (only part surviving), Peninnis Head Lighthouse (though rather badly sited and therefore perhaps a doubtful example), Innisidgen (partly obscured by undergrowth) and Toll's Hill (Figs 24 and 25). Another battery above Bar Point could be of this type but is currently obscured by bracken and brambles. Of these, Church Point, Peninnis Head Lighthouse and Bar Point are in higher locations, but in the case of the first two

Figure 24 (right, above)
Typical of many of the coastal batteries, this structure at Morval Point is located on a spine of rock above low cliffs. The suggested rectangular bivouac platform to the north (above left) does not show up well on this image due to the direction of the light, but the grey hexagonal floor of a Second World War pillbox can be seen at the extreme right.
[NMR 26573/005]

Figure 25 (right, below)
The battery at Morval Point is a V-shaped earthwork fronting a flat platform for the guns. The rectangular earthwork to the north has been described as a 'bivouac platform' contemporary with the battery, but its position and the sharp profile of its scarps suggest that it is a much later feature.

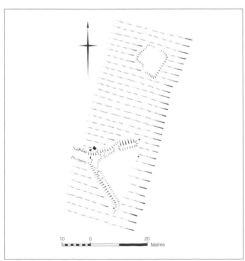

this reflects the nature of the topography on the southern coast of St Mary's. There are two visible batteries on Peninnis Head, the one near the lighthouse being the better preserved; there is allegedly a record of a battery being built at Peninnis during the reign of Queen Anne but which of the two this refers to, or whether it was yet another battery that has been destroyed by the construction of the lighthouse, is uncertain. Morval Point is probably the best preserved of these batteries and appears to have two embrasures surviving in each face. Several of these batteries are said to be associated with 'bivouac platforms'– small terraced areas where the soldiers pitched their tents, or perhaps had wooden huts. Some of these appear to be located in front of batteries and therefore must be regarded as doubtful. In the case of Morval Point the bivouac platform is in advance of the battery and is a crisp earthwork, much sharper than the battery itself, suggesting that it is more recent; it may be the result of 20th-century military activity.

A different, larger type of battery is represented by Carn of Works on the

Gugh beside St Agnes and Pellew's Redoubt on Toll's Island, at the east side of St Mary's (Fig 26). These comprise a full circuit of defence with two gun positions to the front and a narrow entrance at the rear; both show slight traces of defensive outworks.

The battery on Helvear Hill is similar in some respects to these redoubts but is much more massively built (Fig 27). It is the most substantial of all these earthworks with the possible exception of Oliver's Battery on Tresco. The Helvear Hill battery also probably provided two gun positions but it is less symmetrical than Pellew's Redoubt and has a less well-defined back; it has the appearance of an unfinished work. Though the battery itself was cleared of undergrowth in 2008 its immediate surroundings are still overgrown and it is not clear whether there are accompanying outworks or breastworks; early plans suggest that there was a ditch extending to the west.

To the south of Helvear and Toll's Island is Mount Todden (Figs 28, 29 and 30). The battery here is unlike anything else on the islands and it is difficult to find a parallel for it anywhere. A reference in the Parliamentary Survey of 1652 demonstrates that it was in existence by that date. It comprises a massive stone-and-earth bank, roughly triangular in plan, but it lacks a ditch or any obvious quarry as a source for the building material. In the interior is a stone-built structure built partly of large megalithic blocks. It is tempting to suggest that this is the remnant of a chambered tomb and that it is the mound material that forms the rampart of the redoubt. The structure was apparently a watch house or part of a signal station of 18th- or 19th- century date and iron fixings to guy a mast are visible. A hollow in the eastern angle has been described as a gun platform; this may be the case but it clearly cuts into the back of the rampart and is a later feature, possibly related to the Second World War structure in the interior (*see* page 68).

The breastworks around St Mary's are extensive, though perhaps not as extensive as some archaeologists have claimed (Fig 31). Those on the Garrison have been well-studied and authenticated and there are also believable stretches near the blockhouse on the north-eastern side of the island and along the western side of Watermill Cove. The Garrison's breastworks and batteries are the most distinct as in 1715 Christian Lilly had recommended their retention and the repairs to them mean that they have survived better than elsewhere on the island (*see* page 31).

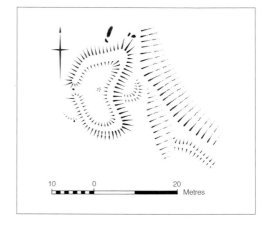

Figure 26
Pellew's Redoubt consists of a substantial earthwork built in the form of two conjoined bastions, with a narrow entrance to the rear and it is similar in form to the battery at Carn of Works on the Gugh. There is little sign of a surrounding ditch. A breastwork can be seen extending to the south-east along the top of the slope that drops to the sea.

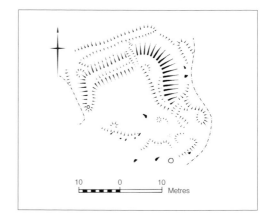

Figure 27
Massive earthwork remains at Helvear, consisting of a rampart and ditch, mark the site of this battery, but the amorphous shape of its south-eastern extremity suggests that it may never have been completed.

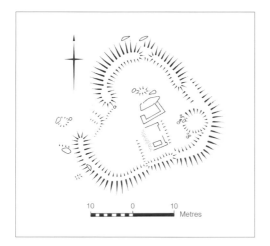

Figure 28 (above)
Without parallel on the islands, Mount Todden battery or fort comprises a substantial bank with an entrance to the west. The central structure is partly megalithic and it is possible that this is a prehistoric tomb that has been drastically modified, the mound material having been pushed out to form the rampart. Documentary evidence suggests that this had happened by 1652. To the south of the central structure are the remains of a Final Responder Beacon from the Second World War. The hollow inside the eastern angle is possibly a small quarry or part of the Beacon's structure.

Figure 29 (above, right)
The earthworks show well in newly cleared pasture in this recent aerial photograph of Mount Todden. In the centre of the fort is the stone-built look-out post with the concrete footings for the Second World War Final Responder Beacon to the left; below this the cut into the back of the rampart can just be seen, which was probably part of the same installation.
[NMR 26579/037]

Figure 30 (right)
This building within Mount Todden Battery, a combination of massive boulders and dry-stone walling, may be the much-modified chamber of a prehistoric tomb. It seems to have been used as a lookout post and signalling station.
[DP085431]

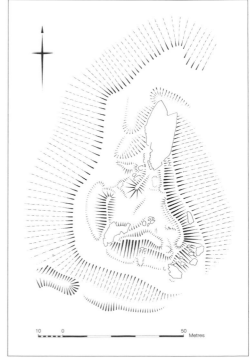

Figure 31
This breastwork, to the south of King Charles' Battery, dates to the Civil War but was repaired in the early 18th century. It is approximately 0.5m high externally; the firing trench is 0.8m deep at present but excavation has shown that its original depth was about 1.3m. [DP022627]

Figure 32
Oliver's Battery, an irregularly shaped battery was built in April 1651 on high ground on the south side of Carn Near, a prominent rock outcrop. It consists of ramparts with external ditches to the west and south. At the north end, tucked under the outcrop, are the footings of a small rectangular building; the gun positions are at the southern end.

Oliver's Battery, at Carn Near on the south end of Tresco, is the only battery that can be convincingly linked to a documented historical event – the capture of Tresco by Blake's forces and the subsequent bombardment of shipping in the Road and St Mary's Pool (Fig 32). To encourage the reluctant Grenville to come to terms, Blake started to build this battery at the end of April 1651. Three guns were mounted in it and the first shot was fired on 4 May; unfortunately the gun exploded, killing two people. On the following day, the remaining guns and a replacement for the one that blew up began to fire in earnest along with guns from the Parliamentarian fleet and, after protracted negotiation, terms of surrender were agreed on 23 May. The earthwork is massive but irregular, conforming to the rock outcrop on which it stands. Claims that it is on the site of a pre-existing battery are not convincing; other earthworks in the area seem to be the remains of hollow ways and sandpits. The gun positions can be made out at the southern extremity of the battery while the footings of a small rectangular building, possibly a magazine, survive at the northern end, close under the rock of Carn Near itself.

Apart from Oliver's Battery, there is no firm dating evidence for any of the other works described above. The widely held view that they are predominantly the work of Grenville during his two and a half years as

Governor may be correct but it is important to stress that this is not proven. Some of them could be earlier; Parliament had voted £1,000 for the defence of Scilly when it controlled the islands in 1646–8. Some may be later, during the Dutch Wars of the later 17th century or the War of the Spanish Succession in the reign of Queen Anne; there is allegedly documentary evidence for the construction of at least one battery at that time.

The only building that can be securely attributed to the civil wars is Cromwell's Castle. In the Parliamentary Survey of 1652 it was described as a 'new blockhouse' and in 1715 Christian Lilly provided a more detailed description (Fig 33):

> Standing at the Foot of a Steep hill much higher than its Top, and is a Huge Mass of Masonry, consisting of a Round Tower two Storys high, with a Platform for six Gunns upon it, and a Battery before it for Six more at the Watters Edge.[14]

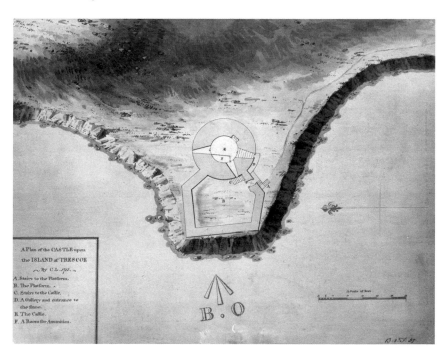

Figure 33
In 1715 Christian Lilly surveyed Cromwell's Castle and found that the structure, only 60 years old, was still serviceable though in need of repairs. The plan shows the attached gun platform that was reworked in the 1740s.
[NMR WORKS 31/1143]

Figure 34
Standing on a large rock at the mouth of New Grimsby Harbour on Tresco, the tower and the attached gun platform of Cromwell's Castle would have bristled with artillery aimed at preventing hostile forces using the sheltered anchorage.
[NMR 23933/027]

Figure 35
Comparing the stonework on the outside of the tower of Cromwell's Castle with the plan of 1715, it is clear that the means of entering the structure has changed. Originally there was also an access through the tower's seemingly odd window in its south side, where a ledge still projects.
[DP085002]

A blockhouse seems to have been on this site since the 16th century, but the new element of the 1650s was the tall, cylindrical tower which contained some heated domestic accommodation inside with a gun platform on the rooftop commanding the bay (Figs 34, 35, and 36). This tower is widely acknowledged as an oddity. Firm documentary evidence seems to contradict its architectural style and details, which would be more suitable for the 1550s rather than the 1650s. Beside the tower there is a lower gun platform which was apparently rebuilt in the 1740s but may be a revamping of an earlier structure.

On 29 May 1660 Charles II arrived triumphantly in London to take the throne and by Christmas 1660 the army of the Commonwealth had been largely abolished. Edward Sherburne was commissioned on 27 December 1660 to report on the arms and defences of the main fortifications in the south-west of England. In the first part of his manuscript, submitted on 20 August 1661,

Figure 36
Now just an empty platform, the top of Cromwell's Castle in the 1650s would have been a hive of activity if it had ever been attacked. Beside the openings for the guns, the small sockets for the ropes that controlled the recoil of the guns can still be seen.

he examined Scilly. On St Mary's there were 5 culverins, 18 demi-culverins, 41 sakers, 22 minions and two 3-pounders that were serviceable and 7 various guns that were unusable. The vast majority of gun carriages (82 out of 95) were inadequate. On Tresco there were 9 guns and none had serviceable carriages.

In addition to reporting on armaments he provided recommendations on repairs to buildings and defences that were needed, though it seems that the largest items were never undertaken. Star Castle needed repairs to its roof, entrance, portcullis and floors and some batteries were to be provided with new timber guardhouses or were to have the existing ones repaired. Repairs were also needed to the storehouse, the blockhouse near Innisidgen and to the smith's forge. There was also an item for repairs and new roofs for the soldiers' lodgings, the Folly, which was at the south end of the Garrison. Sherburne's largest recommendation was a substantial repair and reconstruction programme for the earthwork defences around the Garrison that would have cost over £5,000. On Tresco he recommended repairs to Cromwell's Castle, King Charles' Castle (which was used as soldiers' lodgings) and the Old Blockhouse and its surrounding earthworks.

Christian Lilly's survey

In 1715 Christian Lilly visited the Isles of Scilly as part of his investigation into the fortifications of the Plymouth Division. He was one of seven engineers dispatched to complete surveys of their allotted regions as part of the major reforms of the Board of Ordnance undertaken by the Duke of Marlborough. The backdrop to the reforms was the signing of the Treaty of Utrecht in 1713 which ended more than a decade of European conflict, the accession of George I and the election of a Whig Government in 1714, and the first Jacobite rebellion in 1715.

Lilly was charged with surveying, repairing and improving the defences of Portland, Dartmouth, Plymouth, Falmouth and the Isles of Scilly. The manuscript he compiled is now deposited in the British Library. It consists of a short introduction, a map of the Garrison with a view of the islands, a number of architectural drawings of proposed buildings inside the Garrison and a

Figure 37
In four of the eight angles of the parapet of Star Castle small barracks buildings were created for soldiers. They were repaired by Lilly after 1715 and three today are available as accommodation. The fourth has not been repaired and so its modest corner fireplace is still visible. [DP085306]

detailed table outlining the work that would be required to make the fortifications serviceable.

Lilly revealed that all the defences on the islands, particularly on the Garrison, were in a poor state of repair. He said that: 'for besides what Accommodations and Conveniences are in the Castle, it Self, there has been two large Storehouses, Severall Guard-houses, and many Barracks, with other Offices fitt to receive and accommodate, a Considerable number of men, all of which have been built at great Expence, but are now so many heaps of Ruines.'[15] The castle required repairs totalling £121 9s 9d and the three barracks or 'little lodging rooms' on the ramparts of the castle were ruinous (Fig 37 and *see* Fig 15). Their reinstatement would cost £92 4s 2½d to carry out and this appears to have taken place.

Lilly suggested converting the old guardhouse and storehouse into barracks with 20 bedsteads. However, he also felt that further accommodation was needed to house 120 men and he provided a design for this barrack building, though it was never built. A guardhouse at Steval Point was beyond repair and he recommended that it should be replaced by a new building. Lilly proposed the construction of a storehouse that was located overlooking Newman's Rock. This five-bay, stone building was constructed and survives today as Newman House. In style it is very similar to the buildings flanking the slightly earlier gate of Pendennis Castle in Cornwall. Lilly also concluded that the Master Gunner should have his own house within the Garrison rather than having to live in Hugh Town. He proposed and built a small three-bay, lobby-entry house containing two rooms on the ground floor with a central stair leading to an attic that probably contained two bedrooms. This house is now known as the White House.

After addressing the buildings within the Garrison, Lilly turned his attention to the walls and earthworks. He estimated that the total cost of the work would be £598 1s 7d for sodwork and £375 1s 5d for earthwork, though by reusing some material the total cost could be reduced to £879 7s 7¾d. Some parts of the stone walls also required significant repairs. The left flank and most of the face of Newman's Battery had disappeared and to repair this would cost £93 12s 0d. The south-west corner of the Lower Benham Battery had collapsed leaving a large breach between 40ft and 50ft long (12–15m), a repair that would cost £40 to correct (*see* Fig 85).

Included in Lilly's report is a beautiful and very detailed map of the Garrison (Fig 38). This recorded that the fortifications were in stone from the ruinous Newman's Battery in the north to the Lower Broom Battery south of Upper Benham Battery. Thereafter, there were stone bastions at Morning Point, Woolpack Battery, Bartholomew Battery, Steval Battery and King Charles' Battery. Since the first map of the Garrison was created in 1655 the changes to the stone fortifications had been modest. The major alteration was that stone walls had been built from Upper Benham to Lower Broom and between Newman's Battery and the Well Platform.

Although Lilly spent most of his time on St Mary's, he briefly visited Tresco. At New Grimsby he described what he saw at the harbour and was of the opinion that Cromwell's Castle would need repairs amounting to £55 18s 7d. Lilly also visited the Old Blockhouse at Old Grimsby which 'is also very much decayed having nothing but the walls standing, yet I think it ought to be repaired'. To achieve this £28 0s 8d would need to be allocated.

Lilly also provided a detailed list of the guns available to defend the Garrison. These ranged from a handful of 3-pounders to two 12-pounders and three 16-pounders. However, as well as these probably relatively modern guns, Lilly recorded the presence of more archaic types of artillery piece, including 8 'W Culverins', 20 demi-culverins, 24 minions and 7 sakers. Although he found 89 guns in the Garrison and 31 elsewhere in the islands, he had to recommend providing 101 new gun carriages, an indication of the poor state of maintenance of the cannons. Lilly estimated that £620 0s 9d would need to be spent on this and on 5 August 1718 Portsmouth dockyard was instructed to provide oak carriages mounted on plank wheels for three 18-pounders, fourteen 9-pounders, eleven 5¼-pounders and eighteen 4-pounders. The provision of 46 new carriages falls short of the 101 recommended by Lilly but probably reflects the true number of reasonably serviceable pieces of artillery available on the islands.

On 13 March 1715/6 £1,000 was allocated to Scilly, a large sum compared to the £500 being spent on St Mawes, Plymouth and Portland, but modest compared to the £2,500 needed for Portsmouth, Guernsey and Jersey, and Sheerness and Tilbury. On 18 May 1716 a separate instruction was given to Colonel Lilly to spend £825 19s 3¼d and there was a further large request for an imprest to pay a bill of £456 21s (sic) dated 23 August 1716. Lilly had suggested

Figure 38
In 1715 Christian Lilly surveyed the state of Scilly's defences and included in his report a very detailed plan of the Garrison and a view of Hugh Town, the Garrison and Star Castle from Buzza Hill. On the plan the existing walls were shown with a pink outer line while both sides of the earthworks are in black. [©The British Library Board, KING\'S 45 f7]

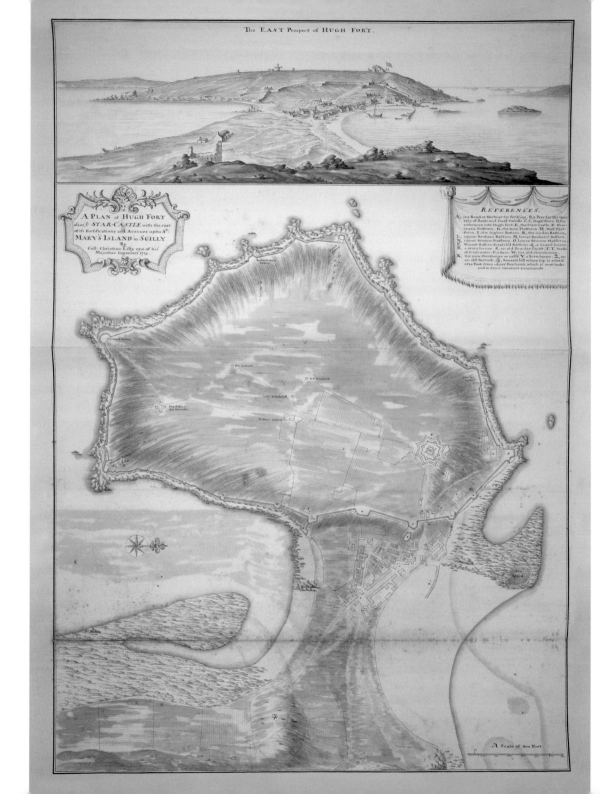

The EAST Prospect of HUGH FORT.

A PLAN of HUGH FORT
alias y^e STAR-CASTLE with the rest
of it's Fortifications and Avenues upon S^t.
MARY'S ISLAND in SCILLY
By
Coll. Christian Lilly one of his
Majesties Ingeniers 1715.

REFERENCES.

A Scale of 600 Foot.

that £3,914 1s 3d would be the whole cost of his scheme but the barracks which would have cost £1,304 3s 2½d was not built. In 1717 Lilly returned to the islands, presumably to inspect the completed works, and after this Scilly returned to being a minor player in the papers of the Board of Ordnance.

The Garrison between 1715 and 1740

The Board of Ordnance's resident man in Scilly between 1714 and the late 1750s was Abraham Tovey. He appears in papers before Lilly's survey and prior to this he had served in the artillery train in Spain from 1706 until 1713. He is described in various documents as Storekeeper and as Master Gunner in Scilly. As Storekeeper he managed the everyday needs of the garrison and carried out minor repairs to buildings, while wearing his other hat he normally commanded six gunners. Therefore, each year he drew a regular salary and various monies for expenses depending on the work being carried out (Fig 39).

In the 1720s and 1730s Tovey normally confined his work to minor repairs but in his bill dated 31 December 1728 he included £44 'To Building 32 Perch & ½ of Masonry Worke on Sadlers Battery' and 'Cutting 909 ft of Moor Stone and Laying 1596 ft for ditto'.[16] This was the detached battery in front of the Garrison Gate known as Mount Holles and in the 1738/9 survey of the defences it was described as follows: 'Saddlers Battery has 11 Guns serv'ble but on uns'ble Carriages, the Battery is in good Order.'[17] Despite being 'in good Order' it was not maintained as part of the new defences in the 1740s.

Extending the Garrison Walls in the 1740s

In November 1739 war broke out between Britain and Spain, and this bi-lateral conflict soon merged into a wider European struggle, the War of Austrian Succession that lasted from 1740 until 1748. This war, with its complex background and issues, saw Britain, the Holy Roman Empire, the Dutch Republic and other smaller states lined up against France, Prussia, Spain and

Figure 39
Abraham Tovey was a figure of some importance in the military establishment in Scilly and he masterminded the early parts of the 1740s construction campaign. However, it is debateable whether he actually deserved the accolade of having his initials placed alongside King George II's and the Governor's above the Garrison Gate. [DP085284]

their allies. However, while British and French armies might fight against each other in support of allies, the two countries only went to war formally in 1744, raising the spectre of possible invasion. When the French incursion came, it was in the form of supporting Bonnie Prince Charlie's Jacobite rebellion, which after marching as far south as Derby, ended in ultimate defeat at Culloden on 16 April 1746. The War of Austrian Succession formally ended in October 1748 with the peace treaty signed at Aix-la-Chapelle.

This European conflict, which extended through naval warfare in the colonies to America, the Carribbean and India, was the background to the reconstrucion of a substantial part of the Garrison Walls on St Mary's. Between 1741 and late 1746 or early 1747 substantial walls were built between Lower Broom and Steval Point, as well as from King Charles' Battery to Newman's Platform. Their construction would help to secure Scilly's anchorages thus impairing any action against England from the west, and would help to frustrate support for dissent in Ireland and Scotland.

A series of maps in the National Monuments Record in Swindon and the National Archives in London trace this endeavour, but a more detailed account can be found in the papers of the Board of Ordnance in the National Archives. When these two sources are combined with the evidence of the built fabric, a complex story of distinct campaigns emerges.

 This story of the building of the Garrison Walls begins on 26 August 1739 in the Council Chamber at Whitehall where the Lords of the Privy Council reviewed a memorandum submitted by Sir Francis Godolphin, the Governor of the Isles of Scilly. Accompanying it was a report prepared by Captain Jeffreyson, the Commanding Officer of Scilly. This systematically described the state of the fortifications and included recommendations about what should be done to improve them. The picture that emerges is of batteries in poor repair, guns that were unusable and earthworks in a heavily eroded condition. Jeffreyson recommended work to the batteries, but the earthworks around the south end of the Garrison were beyond repair and probably threatened by coastal erosion as he regularly stated that the batteries and intervening breastworks should be 'retired', ie built further inland.[18]

The Privy Council seems to have been uncertain about the seriousness of the condition of the fortifications, and so one of its engineers, Thomas Armstrong, was sent to conduct an examination. Armstrong submitted an expenses claim to the Board of Ordnance that included the following item: '10 February (1739/40) 58 Days Charges in going to the Islands of Scilly to view & make a Report of the State of works there £17 12s 10½ d.'[19] There is no evidence in the Ordnance papers of his report, but the lack of activity in the financial records in 1740 and the huge increase in activity in 1741 suggest he returned and recommended a major building programme.

From 1741 until early 1747 it is possible to track the development of the construction programme, at least in general terms, by the amount of money being spent. However, due to the methods of financial record-keeping the wealth of figures require considerable analysis and some educated guesswork to make sense of them. Regardless of any confusion over the detailed costs, it is clear that Abraham Tovey spent hundreds of pounds in 1741, compared to between £20 and £100 in the years before major works began. It is also clear that from 1741 work began on the east and north side of the Garrison and proceeded rapidly in a clockwise fashion.

A copy of a 1741 map shows stone walls running from Newman's Platform to Lower Broom with the rest of the circuit defended by earthworks (Fig 40). Substantial, probably stone and sodwork batteries are shown at Morning Point, Woolpack, Bartholomew, Steval Point and King Charles. On the 1741 map a long stretch of the earthworks south of Lower Broome are absent, as if these may have fallen into the sea since 1715.

A 1742 map includes the earthworks along the south side of the Garrison, fragments of which have survived outside the new walls (Fig 41). It also includes the line of proposed new stone defences that were to be added. Existing stone walls are shown between King Charles' Battery and Newman's Platform, demonstrating that this stretch of wall had been built between 1741 and 1742. In style the stonework of this wall is similar to the stretch of wall south of Lower Broom, including the use of firing positions.

The 1742 map also shows the line of the proposed walls. These are shown in broadly the form that they were built but with important differences. Most of the circuit was to be provided with redans with only occasional bastions. In the executed scheme five redans were provided along the south side of the Garrison to complement the batteries at Morning Point, Woolpack, Bartholomew and Boscawen (Fig 42). A large battery was to be built at Steval Point and walls with seven redans were to be created between it and King

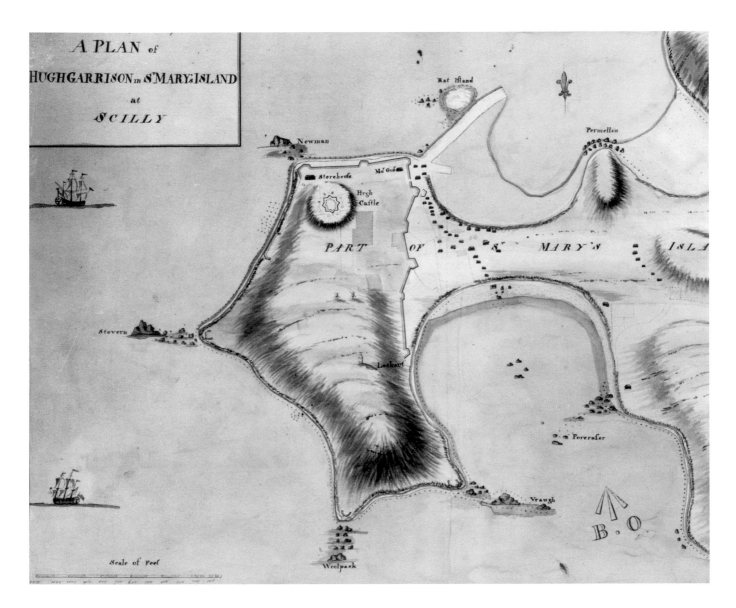

Figure 40
This 1780 copy of a 1741 map shows the Garrison much as it was in 1715 and the original map may have been created in preparation for the major building campaign. Although rather 'artistic' in style, it does seem to be accurate.
[The National Archives, MPH 1/14/5]

Charles. This stretch of wall was to be built some distance inland and consequently uphill from the existing earthworks, perhaps an indication of concern about the stability of the coast. However, walls were never built here and hence the earlier earthworks have survived.

In 1742 Tovey drew and vacated imprests worth £1,195, though some of a large bill entered in the register as relating to 1741 could belong to this year.

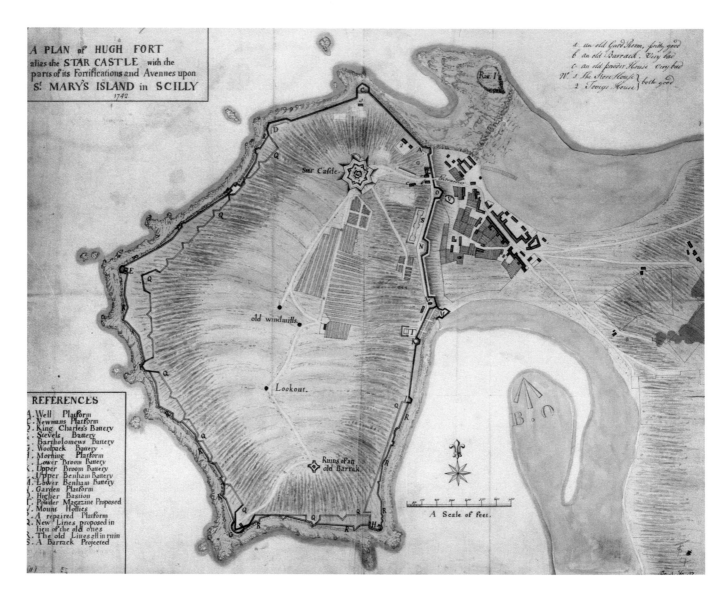

Figure 41 (above)
This map of 1742 shows that walls existed between King Charles' Battery in the north-west of the Garrison and Lower Broom, just to the north of Morning Point in the south-east corner. Elsewhere the Garrison was still enclosed with the earthworks (labelled as R running around the coast). Inside this is the line of the proposed new walls (depicted in yellow and labelled Q).
[NMR WORKS 31/1148]

Figure 42 (right)
Comparing the 1742 map with the section of the Garrison Walls between Woolpack at the top and Morning Point at the bottom it is clear that instead of two redans and an intermediate battery, three redans were built. This photograph also demonstrates the scale of the operation undertaken so rapidly in the 1740s.
[NMR 26571/010]

In 1743 he drew and reconciled imprests worth £1,600, but at the end of the year he also submitted a detailed bill amounting to £1,269 10s 7½ d for the works done to that date. The reason for the sudden appearance of this precise account may have been due to the arrival in Scilly of William Horneck during the second half of the year. Horneck was a very senior engineer having been appointed as Director of Engineers in 1742, the second highest rank in the civil side of the Board of Ordnance.

Tovey's detailed bill in 1743 reveals that since the campaign began, work had been undertaken from Lower Broom to Woolpack, as well as from King Charles' Battery to Newman's Platform. The bill is also instructive as it reveals that the stone for the building work had been quarried on the island. What is unclear is whether Woolpack and the works on the south-east half of the Garrison were completed, but Kane William Horneck's map of 1744 reveals that during that year work had reached a short distance to the west of Redan B, which is to the west of Woolpack (Fig 43). There is a clear joint in the masonry 16.7m west of Redan B on the outside face and 17.4m along the inside face, corresponding to where Horneck's map ends (Fig 44). This interruption is marked further by a contrast in the treatment of drainage holes, with no holes to the east of this joint being equipped with projecting spouts, whereas to its west most examples of drainage spouts occur.

During 1744 Tovey did not draw any imprests, but at the end of the year he submitted a bill for £1,474 16s 0d. Until 1744 Abraham Tovey seems to have been largely unchecked in his management of the building programme. However, from 1745–7 a number of new names appear in the Ordnance accounts – engineers, overseers and two men who seem to have been drafted-in to deal with the finances. William Redstone was described as the 'Assistant Storekeeper at Plymouth & Paymaster to the Works at Scilly Island' while Nicholas Mercator was his successor as 'Pay Master to the Works at Islands of Scilly'.[20] Redstone first appeared in the accounts in April 1745 when he began to draw imprests. After 1745 he only vacated imprests and by 31 March 1746 he was described as the storekeeper at Kinsale. In 1745 Redstone seems to have been managing the finances, but during the summer 'John Hardesty Practioner (sic) [Practitioner] Engineer' was paid £18 16s 0d 'for his Encouragement and in Consideration of his Trouble in carrying on the Works at the Island of Scilly, from the 26th Day of March 1745 to the 30th of September following'.[21]

Figure 43
This map was produced in 1744 by Kane William Horneck, an engineer who was the illegitimate son of William Horneck, the Director of Engineers who had visited the year before. It is important as it shows the progress along the south side of the Garrison to the west of Redan B.
[The National Archives, MPH 1/413]

Figure 44
The 1744 map showed an abrupt end to the walls that matches a change in the detailing of the stonework in the Garrison Walls. To the left can be seen the larger stonework that is characteristic of the later phases of the construction, while heading off towards Redan B the stonework is still good quality but smaller scale and slightly more irregular.
[DP022600]

Figure 45
On the south side of the Garrison between Morning Point and the Woolpack Battery the stone in the wall between Redan C and Redan D is small though well-coursed. This stone seems to have been quarried nearby while Abraham Tovey was in charge of the works, probably in 1742–3.
[DP022527]

Figure 46
The west wall of Redan A reveals that three years later the quality of the stone and the size of the blocks had improved markedly, perhaps due to Abel Croad's involvement from 1745–6. Projecting stone spouts were now in use to drain water away from the foundations of the walls.
[DP022603]

Two other names of significance emerge in the later phases. Isaac Tovey, Abraham's son, was described in 1745 as the Overseer of Works and from 1746 until early 1747, when works finished completely, John Hargrave took over this role.

In 1745 Redstone may have drawn at least £1,000, or more if the later entries for reconciliation are included, and Tovey also drew £500. Redstone also submitted a bill for £1,098 17s 0½d covering work carried out between 30 June and 23 October 1745. The most striking entry in this bill is the £946 9s 8d paid to 'Mr Abel Croad Contractors as per bill of Measuremt'. The identity of Abel Croad is clarified a little in a bill submitted by Mercator on 31 October 1746 in which he is described as a 'Mason'.[22] Unfortunately specifics of his work are absent, though it does say that he was being paid for his 'Bill of Measurement & for Day Labourers' suggesting he provided the labour for construction as well as perhaps being a supplier of stone. Had most of the good stone on the island already been used and was therefore Croad providing stone for the finer outer faces of the walls? (Figs 45 and 46) This interpretation seems to fit with the improved quality of the masonry of the walls in the latest phases of construction, from around Woolpack to Steval.

In 1746 Redstone's successor Nicholas Mercator drew imprests totalling £1,050 and on 31 October 1746 he submitted a substantial bill of £826 9s 1d. During 1746 John Hargrave had succeeded Isaac Tovey as Overseer of the Works, and his last payment for this role ends on 5 May 1747 though the presence of travelling claims within it suggests he had left before this.

A map of 1746, when Mercator was active in Scilly, exists only as an 1810 copy held in the National Monuments Record (Fig 47). Walls with pink shading run from King Charles' Battery clockwise to Boscawen's, while the short section from Boscawen's to Steval Point, including Redan A, is shown with a yellow tone. Does the colour scheme indicate that this piece of wall was not built or was in progress in 1746? Documents confirm that work was drawing to an end in that year and this plan seems to reflect this.

Two of the earlier batteries, which already existed in 1715, were rebuilt during the course of the 1741–6 campaign. Higher Bastion to the south of the Garrison Gate and Jefferson's Battery immediately to the north both have stonework characteristic of the 1744–6 phases (Fig 48). Both appeared on Lilly's survey of 1715 though Jefferson's is just shown as a simple line as if it

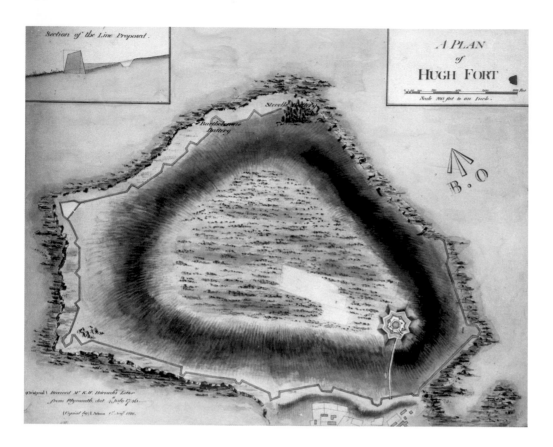

Section of the Line Proposed.

A PLAN
of
HUGH FORT

Scale 200 feet to an Inch.

was incomplete or just an idea being considered. In 1742 it was labelled as a repaired platform and appears on the 1744 and 1750 maps though it is omitted from the 1746 survey.

A map of 1750 in Star Castle shows the abrupt break at Steval Point (Fig 49). It also shows the proposed walls along the west side of the island but these were never built. Thereafter there is no further discussion of extending the walls along the west side of the Garrison.

These various maps show the progress of the walls around the Garrison but they also show how one battery fell out of use. Mount Holles Battery, sometimes referred to as Sadler's Battery, appears on the 1742 map but is omitted in the 1746 version. William Borlase writing in the 1750s said that: 'Just below the Lines are the remains of an old Fort: It is a round hillock and seems to have had a Keep on top of it … the walls of it have been stripp'd to build the Lines; 'tis call'd Mount Holles.'[23] In a panoramic view dated 1752 Borlase shows it just as a small, irregular lump.

Figure 47
This 1810 copy of a 1746 map seems to be by Kane William Horneck, though he did not visit Scilly during that year. It shows the walls as they exist today, but the final stretch of wall from the wrongly labelled Bartholomew Battery (actually Colonel George Boscawen's Battery) to Steval Point is shown in yellow, as if not complete.
[NMR WORKS 31/1149]

Figure 48
Higher Bastion, also known as King George's Battery, is immediately to the south of the Garrison Gate. The site of a bastion since the 17th century it was rebuilt in 1744–6 in neat, large blocks and with projecting spouts.
[DP022362]

Figure 49
This map of 1750 shows the Garrison Walls as they survive today, but it also reveals that there was still an intention to build new walls along the west side of the Garrison, inland from where the earthworks now survive.
[DP022583, Courtesy of Star Castle]

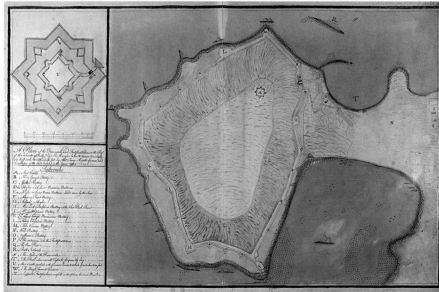

A walk around the Garrison Walls – Excursus

The development of the Garrison Walls can be traced while walking from the gate clockwise around the Garrison. Each of the batteries and redans are labelled and the main ones appear on Map 3 at the end of this book.

1590s

During the 1590s the walls between Well Platform at the north of the Garrison and Upper Benham Battery were built. The gate and the surrounding masonry were rebuilt later, in 1742. This is an obvious insertion into an early stretch of walling, which had large blocks of rubble with small stones packing the wide joints (Fig 50 and *see* Figs 19 and 92).

Figure 50
South of the Garrison Gate there is a small sallyport, giving access into the Garrison, that may date from the original phase of the 1590s. The walls in this earliest phase to the south of the Garrison Gate employ large, irregular blocks in walls with no regular pattern of coursing.
[DP022371]

Civil War

Earthworks were built from Upper Benham Battery all the way round to the north side of the Garrison. Fragments survive outside the walls on the south side of the Garrison, but the best stretch can be seen running along the cliff edge from Steval Point to King Charles' Battery (*see* Fig 31).

1655–1715

After the Civil War the major change was that stone walls were built from Upper Benham southwards to Lower Broom and to connect Newman's Battery to the Well Platform at the north end of the Garrison. The batteries at Lower and Upper Broom had been washed away by 1750 and this stretch of wall seems to have been partly rebuilt later.

1741–2

The first phase of work in the 1740s was the construction in stone of the stretch of wall between King Charles' Battery and Newman's Battery, along the north side of the Garrison (Fig 51).

Figure 51
This section of wall between King Charles' Battery and Newman's Platform dates from 1741–2 and was part of the earliest phase of the major reconstruction campaign. The stone is regularly laid in courses and is more rectangular than in the 1590s, though it lacks the monumentality and quality of the later phases. [DP022513]

1742–3

The second phase of construction stretched from Morning Point to the Woolpack Battery. There is a joint in the east side of the latter battery, marked by a change in the quality of the stonework. The joint in the east wall coincides with a change in wall thickness and the character of the stone changes from regular, small, neat stones of the previous phase to monumental blocks with finer jointing (Figs 52 and 53).

1744

This phase of work stretches from the joint in the wall on the east side of Woolpack Battery to the west side of Redan B. The joint marking the western extremity of this phase corresponds with that depicted on the map drawn in 1744 (Fig 54 and *see* Fig 43).

Figure 52
Morning Point at the south-east corner of the Garrison Walls was built in 1742–3 and is already of a superior quality to the stonework seen along the north side of the Garrison.
[DP022526]

Figure 53
On the south side of the Garrison the stonework of the batteries is sometimes superior to the work in the intermediate walls. The stonework in this section, immediately to the east of Morning Point, is less regular than in the battery. In front were allotments once used by the soldiers of the garrison, but they are now home to wild flowers.
[DP022458]

Figure 54
By the time Woolpack Battery was under way in 1743 and 1744 the stonework was of higher quality, with large, regular blocks in neat courses. However, the drainage spouts of the last phases had yet to make an appearance. On the left side of the east wall the interrupted stonework is due to the insertion of a pillbox during the Second World War.
[DP022475]

1744–5/6

This phase extends from the joint in the wall to the west of Redan B to the west side of Bartholomew Battery, where the shading of the wall in the 1746 map changed from pink to yellow. Higher Bastion to the south of the Garrison Gate and Jefferson's Battery to the north were rebuilt or refaced in this phase or the subsequent one. Drainage spouts are a feature in use by this date (Fig 55 and *see* Fig 47).

1746–early 1747

During this phase the short section of wall from Bartholomew Battery to Steval Point was built. On the 1746 plan it was shown in yellow (Fig 56 and *see* Fig 46).

Figure 55
Bartholomew Battery was built between 1744 and 1746 and while its stonework is of similar quality to Woolpack, it has the drainage spouts employed in the last phases of construction.
[DP022489]

Figure 56
At Steval Point the stately walls of the Garrison ended abruptly in late 1746 or early 1747. Although the 1750 map shows there was still an intention to continue them to King Charles' Battery, they were never completed.
[DP022504]

Napoleonic War

In 1793 Britain went to war with France – a conflict that lasted until 1815 interspersed with only brief interludes of peace. Again the Isles of Scilly were recognised as being of strategic significance but the existing defences seem to have been considered adequate. Troutbeck writing in 1796 was impressed by Scilly's defences:

> This island is defended by a strong garrison, situated upon a peninsula, on the West side of Heugh Town, which it overlooks …. . It contains a company of soldiers, a master gunner, and six other gunners. The barracks are at the entrance into the lines, which being built with moor-stone, make a good appearance; and being flanked with bastions, and salient-angles at proper distances, which were designed to go quite round this peninsula, the whole circuit is about a mile and a half. [24]

Figure 57
King Charles' Battery at the north end of the Garrison was in existence in 1741. Its mixture of stone and sodwork may suggest the form of the earliest batteries, before their replacement in the 1740s. With the outbreak of war with France in 1793 the still formidable defences of the Garrison were rearmed, including the provision here of a traversing platform.
[DP022511]

Figure 58
A reconstruction of the only surviving traversing platform in King Charles' Battery – though there may have been another at the western extreme of the Garrison Walls, probably in Boscawen Battery. A 1793 drawing of this arrangement appears in a manuscript held by the Royal Artillery though it was being designed to install on gun towers.

Troutbeck's description included the guns that were in each battery, information that might have been of use to the enemy if it was accurate. The entire circuit bristled with twenty-five 4-pounders, six 6-pounders, nineteen 9-pounders, four 18-pounders and four 24-pounders (Figs 57 and 58).

With the outbreak of war with France in 1793 the number of troops manning the Garrison was increased. The complement of 24 invalids was bolstered by islanders recruited into the Corps of Land Fencibles and by 1795 75 regular non-commissioned officers (NCOs) and men had been brought from the mainland. Despite these reinforcements the population of Hugh Town in 1796 was only around 800 inhabitants, and therefore it could not have mustered a major force if required to resist an enemy attack.

To strengthen Scilly's defences Major Daniel Lyman proposed the construction of three gun towers in 1803, each armed with a 32-pounder carronade on top. The presence of three towers on St Mary's, in the heart of the Garrison, on Buzza Hill and at Newford Down, has led some writers to link them to Lyman's proposal. However, his proposal was never enacted and the three towers have different origins. The tower in the Garrison was one of a pair of windmills, the site of the other being located in bushes nearby. In the 19th century it was repaired and rebuilt to serve as a signal station (*see* Fig 61). Buzza Tower was a new windmill built in 1820 and restored in the early 20th century.

The tower on Newford Down, now known as Telegraph Tower, was built in 1814 to serve as an Admiralty Telegraph Station but it had closed by 1816 (Fig 59). This tower replaced a signal station established on St Martin's in 1804, which survives in a ruinous state (Fig 60). It consisted of a small, three-roomed building, set within a square compound that contained two other small buildings, probably a privy and a store. This compound was soon enlarged and two ancillary buildings and an animal enclosure were created. These modest structures would have been vital to provide even basic comforts for those manning this remote, often inhospitable site.

Figure 59 (above)
In the heart of St Mary's an Admiralty telegraph station was established in 1814 but closed within two years. This was in use by the coastguards by the early 20th century.
[DP085372]

Figure 60 (left)
In the north-east corner of St Martin's, immediately beneath the day mark, a signal station was established in 1804. This bleak, isolated location meant that some modest, domestic accommodation and ancillary buildings were provided for the men who staffed the station.
[NMR 23932/027]

The defences in the 19th century

During the war with France the garrison was never required to fire a shot in anger, and with the defeat of Napoleon, the islands returned to their status as a quiet military backwater. This in turn led to neglect and less than a decade after the threat from France had ceased, George Woodley writing in 1822 recorded the already parlous state of the defences. The state of disrepair suggests that although the garrison had been reinforced during the war with France, little was probably done to improve or even maintain the walls. After Trafalgar the threat from the French fleet had waned, along probably with any appetite to spend money on the defences of Scilly.

Three decades later, Walter White visiting in 1855 described the quiet life of the garrison:

> Then up to Star Castle, past the guard-house at the gate, where you may have a chat with the half-dozen invalids who constitute the garrison. Their duties do not appear to be onerous; among them are hauling the Union Jack up and down, and ringing the bell every three hours, from six in the morning till nine at night.[25]

The garrison was disbanded in 1863, leaving a single elderly caretaker to look after the defences. No-one would have predicted that within a generation this sleepy backwater would again be considered a front line in Britain's defences.

Defended ports

With the development and refinement of the breech-loading gun in the third quarter of the 19th century, the firepower of ships increased dramatically. Existing fortifications were rendered vulnerable and a new approach to defences was required. An 1886 memorandum prepared by Major-General Sir Andrew Clarke, Inspector-General of Fortifications, stated that defences would be blended into the landscape and should avoid any prominent, regular shapes in their design. Guns should be dispersed rather than being concentrated in a large structure and earthwork defences would be preferable to iron and steel.

As well as changing the form of fortifications, the Government also reviewed the location of defences. In 1882 the Morley Committee investigated the defences of mercantile ports as the Government had realised that the country and its navy was wholly dependent on coal. This prompted the creation of a series of defended ports, but the idea of creating a protected anchorage for shipping was extended to Scilly. Therefore, two large batteries with a barracks between were created above the 18th-century Woolpack Battery overlooking St Mary's Sound and these were supplemented by a pair of Defence Electric Lights (DEL) and a small quick-firing (QF) battery at Steval Point (Fig 61). At Bant's Carn in the north of St Mary's another QF battery was created. All these new fortifications followed well-established military forms and therefore could be built quickly with the minimum of pre-planning.

The authorisation for the erection of the large batteries was granted on 24 May 1898 and work began on 2 August 1898. Work was completed on 30 May 1901 having cost £19,800. The new batteries were called Woolpack and Steval and each had a pair of the recently introduced Mark VII 6-in breech-loading guns, which had a range of 12,600yds (11.5km) (Figs 62 and 63).

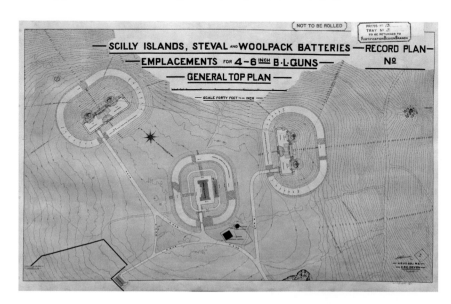

Figure 61
This survey drawing of 1902 shows the completed pair of gun batteries with the barracks block between. Below the barracks can be seen the tower of the signal station – a refurbished old windmill and not a gun tower of the early 19th century. The site of the second old windmill is shown a short distance to the left.
[The National Archives, MPHH/1162/1]

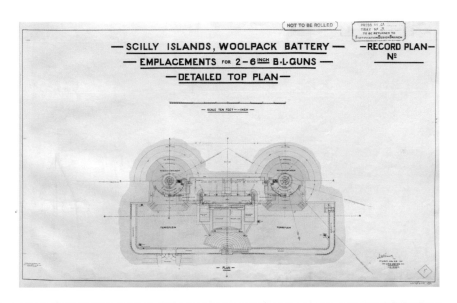

Figure 62 (right)
In this 1902 plan of Woolpack Battery, between the pair of 6-in guns were three subterranean shell stores, two cartridge stores, an artillery store and a small shelter. A series of lifts are shown for raising shells and cartridges up to the guns.
[The National Archives, MPHH/1162/4]

Figure 63 (below)
Woolpack Battery – on top of the Garrison this new large battery would have been a formidable threat to enemy shipping. In the top right is part of the 1740s Garrison Walls.
[NMR 26571/035]

Figure 64 (above)
Beneath this seemingly rural scene, with ponies grazing on an earth bank, is located the Woolpack Battery. A new philosophy of fortification design in the late 19th century meant that defences would be blended into the landscape to delay detection.
[DP085332]

Figure 65 (left)
Woolpack and Steval Batteries were armed with two 6-in guns set in concrete emplacements. The guns were installed for a brief period in the batteries, but were soon removed.
[DP085204]

Each gun was housed in a concrete emplacement within sloping earthworks (Figs 64 and 65). Magazines beneath and between the pair of gun positions were able to hold 1,000 rounds, suggesting preparations for a major conflict. At the rear of each battery was a Depression Position Finder to calculate the position of the guns' targets.

The barracks between the two gun batteries were set within an earthwork similar to the batteries (Fig 66). Behind the barracks there is a separate parallel block containing stores and earth closets. At the south end of this pair of buildings there is a small observation building overlooking the earthworks. This is not an original feature but was designed in July 1905 as a 'Fire Commander's Post' for observing movements in St Mary's Sound and directing fire on targets from all four guns on the island (Fig 67).[26] This demonstrates that if all the guns had been installed they could have been controlled from this single location.

Figure 66 (below)
This small building was to be used as accommodation for the two NCOs who took charge of each battery. In wartime it would be used as a barracks for the 24 men and two NCOs who would man the batteries. [DP085319]

Figure 67 (below, right)
Set behind the barracks this small structure has a window looking out over the earthworks. It was designed as a 'Fire Commander's Post' in July 1905 and surprisingly was built just before the batteries were decommissioned, possibly in the following year. [DP085321]

While the large batteries were under construction, the decision was taken to provide Defence Electric Lights to illuminate any potential enemy shipping in St Mary's Sound. A drawing dated 11 June 1900 was prepared by Lt Col FS Leslie, the commanding officer of the Royal Engineers on the islands. It shows the layout of the cabling required to link the generators inside a sunken structure within Boscawen's Battery to the lights at Steval Point and in front of 18th-century Woolpack Battery.

The two DEL positions are small D-shaped concrete buildings originally with iron shutters (Fig 68). These could be opened to create a directed, concentrated beam of light towards a target and be altered to follow its progress. In the floor of the structure at Woolpack there is a rectangular footprint and a channel where the searchlight and its electrical supply were

Figure 68
A large searchlight was installed inside this small, concrete DEL position in front of the 18th-century Woolpack Battery. The tracks for the shutters that directed the light survive around the main opening in the structure.
[DP022476]

Figure 69
On the hillside between the 18th-century Woolpack and its c 1900 successor above, this small Position Finder Station set into the ground would have identified targets and tracked their movement with the help at night of the DEL.
[DP085220]

located, but in the floor of the position at Steval Point there are no similar indications that the light was ever installed. To control the lights an Electric Light Directing Station on the hillside above the 18th-century Woolpack Battery was created and during the Second World War this was used as an observation post (Fig 69). A similar one behind the Steval Point DEL position later became a small pillbox.

The large 6-in gun batteries were to deal with large, relatively slow-moving targets, but small, fast torpedo boats were thought to be a significant new threat being developed by the French. To counter these boats, quick-firing (QF) guns were created, firing perhaps 25 to 30 rounds per minute. In Scilly two batteries were built, each intended to house two 12-pounder QF guns, which had a range of 8,000yds (7.3km). These batteries were established at Steval Point, on top of the slope above where the 18th-century walls terminate and at

Bant's Carn at the north end of St Mary's (Fig 70). These sites were presumably chosen as they could control either end of the Road, at the heart of Scilly's safe anchorage. Steval Point has a datestone of 1904 while the battery at Bant's Carn is dated 1905. Design drawings for both batteries survive in the National Archives, with the Steval Point drawings being dated May 1903. They were smaller versions of the two larger batteries with a pair of gun positions flanking subterranean stores but with a small, flat-roofed accommodation building beside each battery.

Even before the Bant's Carn datestone was in place, the world had changed in military terms, causing a re-evaluation of Britain's and Scilly's defence. The signing of the *Entente Cordiale* meant that centuries of hostility with France ended and British concerns now turned to the growing might of Germany. Therefore, geographically the east side of England became of greater importance while the south-west was thought to be less vulnerable. The launching of HMS *Dreadnought* in 1906, with its increased firepower and armament, also raised questions about many of the existing coastal defences. In response to these factors a committee was established under General Sir

Figure 70
Similar in form to the larger gun batteries, Steval Point's quick-firing battery would have housed two smaller calibre guns in its concrete emplacements.
[DP085183]

John Owen to consider where coastal defences should be concentrated and the guns that should be provided at these sites. The impact of these changes in Scilly was that the newly created large batteries were soon disarmed, certainly before 1914, and the two QF batteries never had their guns installed. Again Scilly continued its tradition of building impressive fortifications but never firing a shot in anger.

Scilly in the First World War

During the First World War Scilly remained of strategic significance but for an entirely new form of warfare. A naval sub-base was established at St Mary's with a flotilla of Admiralty tugs, armed trawlers and drifters for anti-submarine patrols – but it was in aerial warfare that Scilly made its mark. The start of unrestricted submarine warfare by the Germans at the beginning of 1917 led to an expansion in the establishment of anti-submarine air bases around the coasts of Britain. Even before the outbreak of war it had been discovered that aircraft and airships were of value in hunting submarines; a periscope wake could be seen from several miles away by an airborne observer and in clear conditions the hull of a submerged submarine at periscope depth could be visible from the air. In the event it proved difficult with the technology then available for aircraft or airships to attack submarines successfully. However, they could effectively guide and direct attacks by surface vessels; aircraft were therefore feared by submariners. Aircraft patrolling the sea lanes or escorting convoys would force submarines to dive deep and therefore severely limit their ability to attack shipping. The establishment of a flying boat and seaplane base in Scilly extended the operating range of the Royal Naval Air Service (and subsequently the RAF) far out into the Western Approaches.

An attempt to construct an airship station at Holy Vale, St Mary's, was abandoned and Scilly was instead covered by airships based at Mullion, though they were sometimes moored temporarily in the islands. There was also apparently an observation-balloon base in the Garrison but no permanent structures seem to have been built in connection with this. In January 1917 the flying boat and seaplane base was established at

Porthmellon, despite the warnings of locals that the bay was too exposed. These warnings proved to be well founded and before it became operational the base was moved to a new home at New Grimsby, Tresco (Fig 71). This consisted of a slipway, hangars, offices, ratings' and officers' quarters, a canteen and a sick bay. It was equipped initially with Curtis 'Large America' flying boats and Short 184 seaplanes, and subsequently with improved 'Felixstowe' flying boats and later versions of the Short seaplane. On 18 August 1918 the unit became 234 Squadron RAF.

The first patrol was flown on 28 February 1917 and on 18 May 1917 a flying boat from Scilly flew the first escort over a convoy, an inbound one from the Mediterranean. In the last two years of the war, aircraft from Scilly made 13 U-boat sightings and attacked on nine occasions. The most dramatic incident occurred on 27 May 1917 when the crew of a 'Large America' flying boat saw a U-boat on the surface off Bryher. Unusually, the U-boat fired at the flying boat before diving, holing the aircraft's starboard radiator. The flying boat dropped two bombs, scoring what they believed to be a direct hit. Observers on shore confirmed that the U-boat's stern rose out of the water at an angle of 60° before it sank. The flying boat's radiator was leaking badly and one of the crew climbed onto the wing to plug the hole with a handkerchief. The 'kill' was confirmed at the time and the flying boat's crew were all awarded medals but subsequent research has suggested that the U-boat may have survived the attack.

Nothing apparently survives of the abortive airship moorings at Holy Vale or of the first flying-boat base at Porthmellon, with the exception of a concrete hangar base at the latter. Of the base at Tresco, which was very extensive, covering the whole southern part of New Grimsby Bay, little now remains (Fig 72). The Bothy, a former potato store used for bomb storage, is extant despite being damaged in an explosion. The power house, another former agricultural building converted for the use of the air base, also survives. The iron rails on the slipway reflect where the flying boats and seaplanes were launched and recovered on trolleys, and concrete standings for buildings between the Great Pool and the shore can still be seen (Fig 73). An iron stanchion on Hulman Rock at the south end of the New Grimsby Channel is said to be the remains of a light installation placed to assist aircraft landing in the dark.

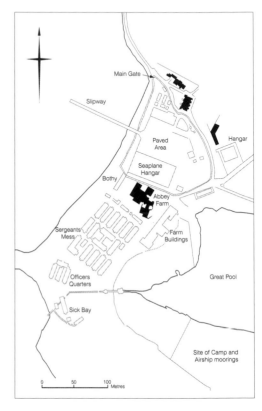

Figure 71
This is a simplified version of an original plan of the seaplane base at New Grimsby, Tresco, showing the main structures clustered around the earlier farmstead. It is based on a drawing by Nigel Plevin in J P Osborne's 'Scillonian War Diary 1914–1918' in the Isles of Scilly Museum.

Figure 72
This modern photograph shows the site of the flying boat and seaplane base on Tresco. Many of the buildings of Abbey Farm remain largely unchanged but the only buildings directly associated with the base are the power house, marked by its substantial chimney, and the bomb store in front of it, parallel with the shore. To the right the concrete footings of some of the accommodation blocks are visible.
[NMR 26581/028]

Figure 73
The original slipway of the New Grimsby air station was of timber; launching and recovery trolleys for the seaplanes ran on the iron rails, reset in the modern slipway.
[DP085121]

Scilly in the Second World War

In military terms Scilly was under-prepared for the Second World War. Civilian preparations were well in hand – gas masks and stirrup pumps had been distributed, air-raid sirens installed and shelters built in 1939. However, in the summer of 1940 the islands were defended by just one Independent Company of troops, with their HQ at Star Castle, and there were no anti-aircraft defences and no significant naval presence.

The islands first saw hostile action on 21 August 1940 when enemy aircraft bombed the Radio Direction Finding Station (RDF) on Peninnis Head. This was followed by several more 'raids', though in fact many of these were probably German crews opportunistically jettisoning their bomb loads (Fig 74). The installation at Peninnis seems to have been a genuine target as it was attacked several times and eventually destroyed just over a year after the first attack. A raid on 29 August 1940 seems to have been particularly worrying and the situation in Scilly was discussed by the War Cabinet on the following day. Winston Churchill declared that the islands must be held 'at all costs' and the Chiefs of Staff were directed to make dispositions accordingly.[27] Meanwhile two destroyers were anchored in St Mary's Pool to give some anti-aircraft cover. On 2 September the Chiefs of Staff decided to double the garrison on the islands to two Independent Companies (approximately 1,000 men) and to provide two Bofors anti-aircraft guns. They also noted that the Newford RDF station was being established but that the aerodrome was small and had been 'rendered useless' (though this does not seem to have been true, in fact).[28] The Bofors guns were delivered and put in position on the following day.

Air raids continued through the early part of 1941, with Telegraph Tower and the adjacent RAF Newford along with Peninnis being the main targets. Newford was a Ground Controlled Interception Station for guiding fighters to intercept enemy bombers and Air Sea Rescue flying boats to ditched aircraft; it had four radio masts and a 360° revolving radar dish on a gantry as well as several huts and a small motor transport section.

By 1941 it was necessary to improve the air defences of the islands. On 19 May 1941 a flight of six Hawker Hurricanes from 87 Squadron RAF, later designated 1449 Flight, landed at the aerodrome. Within an hour of their arrival a German seaplane was spotted, one of the Hurricanes was scrambled

Figure 74
During the Second World War the Luftwaffe published a dossier of images of potential targets and navigation marks, including Scilly. Due to its limited access to British sites, it seems to have relied heavily on photographs from magazines to illustrate key features of the islands.

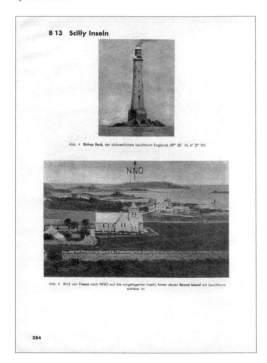

Figure 75
On the aprons of the c 1900 Woolpack Battery are the
bases for the twin masts for the 'RACON' installation
established at the Woolpack Battery in 1943.
[DP085199]

and shot it down. The aerodrome runways were extended and a hangar was built in 1942, but all the buildings were of a temporary nature and the last surviving buildings were demolished in the 1990s. German air raids on the islands continued, though increasingly they were intercepted by the islands' fighters and several bombers were shot down. By early 1942 the Luftwaffe had declared a 90 mile-radius zone around Scilly which was to be avoided in daylight and there were no further air raids.

In 1941 the beaches and military installations were wired and nearly 30 pillboxes were built around the coast of St Mary's. From May 1941 Naval Motor Torpedo Boats were stationed in St Mary's Pool. St Mary's also became a base for RAF and Naval rescue launches and an emergency base for RAF Coastal Command flying boats, with moorings in the harbour and in Porthcressa. Also by 1941 a secret experimental torpedo unit was established on St Martin's and a floating target was moored in Crow Sound. There was also a rifle range and air gunnery range at Giant's Castle.

In 1943 an experimental 'RACON' Beacon was established at the Woolpack Battery by a Canadian RAF unit (Fig 75). The beacon consisted of an antenna

Figure 76
In the foreground is the concrete generator base within the Mount Todden Battery for the Final Responder Beacon installed during the Second World War. This was a blind-flying aid for aeroplanes approaching the airfield.
[DP085429]

on an 8.5m high wooden mast and a transmitter powered by a generator (all duplicated in case of damage or malfunction). The generators were installed in one of the gun emplacements and the operators lived in the underground store. This equipment broadcast a continuous pattern of 'dots' that aircraft navigators used to fix their position.

In April 1944 'technical' work was undertaken at Mount Todden. In a letter to the Air Ministry the Duchy's Land Steward noted that the battery 'is presumed to be an ancient monument' and expressed 'our desire that it should not be touched if at all possible'.[29] However, a generator and other equipment for a Final Responder Beacon, a landing aid for aircraft, were established in the battery beside the small 'lookout' structure (Fig 76 and *see* Figs 29 and 30).

Though the air raids had stopped there were numerous other incidents in and around the islands, including running agents to and from occupied France in small boats from Tresco. On 12 August 1943 one of the Hurricanes tragically crashed into the masts of the *Scillonian*, the islands' regular mainland ferry, and the pilot was killed; on 23 February 1944 a Liberator crash-landed near the aerodrome and while all the crew were saved by the pilot's skill, he was killed by a fragment of broken propeller that flew into the cockpit. There was also some naval activity around the islands and on 20 June 1944 HMS *Warwick* was sunk off the islands by U-413.

After D-Day any serious threat to the islands receded and therefore on 17 September 1944 the Hurricanes were withdrawn and in December Star Castle was de-commissioned. U-boats continued to operate around the islands with some success and a merchant ship was torpedoed off Scilly on 12 January 1945. However, they were under increasing pressure and the final wartime incident around Scilly was the sinking of U-681 by a Liberator off Mincarlo on 11 March 1945.

Much effort was expended after the war in clearing up the miles of barbed wire and other military paraphernalia, so very little now remains of the physical structures of the conflict. The rifle and air gunnery range at Giant's Castle survives as earthworks and there are concrete machine bases at Mount Todden Battery and Deep Point (Fig 77), though the latter partly relate to a post-war Rotor VHF Fixer Station. There is also a large concrete arrow, flush with the ground, near Deep Point, which is probably a direction arrow for the Crow Sound target; this arrow and some accompanying structures are visible on an aerial photograph in the National Monuments Record taken in December 1940. A square earthwork hollow, 2.3m across, with an elaborate covered

Figure 77
The arrow on Normandy Down provides direction to the aerial bombing range, with its moored floating target in Crow Sound off the north-east coast of St Mary's.
[DP085425]

entrance, was uncovered during scrub clearance in 2010 between Carn Morval and Halangy Point; this is possibly a Second World War observation post or machine gun emplacement covering a gap between pillbox positions.

It is the pillboxes around St Mary's, however, that survive best. Some of them were deliberately demolished and some have suffered severe damage from the sea, but about nine are well preserved and fragments of another seven can be seen. The best preserved are at Morning Point, Woolpack, Upper Benham and Steval Point on the Garrison, cunningly worked into pre-existing 18th-century structures. Elsewhere on St Mary's there are examples at Porthloo, Porth Hellick, Tolman Point (which interestingly faces away from the sea), beneath Schooners Hotel overlooking Town Beach and at Old Town, where two well-concealed examples still cover the harbour (Figs 78, 79, 80, and 81). Of the fragmentary pillbox remains, the most evocative is that at

Figure 78 (below, left)
The Cat's Coffin pillbox, disguised as a wall affords a clear field of fire across Old Town Bay. This was designed to operate in conjunction with another pillbox, 140m to the west, the pillbox on Tolman Point and probably other defensive measures including mobile units.
[DP085393]

Figure 79 (below)
The desire to conceal strong points was often met by building them into pre-existing structures. This pillbox in the tip of the 18th-century Woolpack Battery was built of concrete blocks, but faced with granite to blend in with the 18th-century work.
[DP022480]

Figure 80
This pillbox at Tolman Point, of standard hexagonal design, has a defended entrance. This is on the seaward side probably because the rocks would have prevented enemy landings anywhere but in the bays to either side. It may have been designed to operate with other strong points and defensive measures to create a 'killing ground' in Old Town Bay.
[DP085386]

Figure 81
The pillbox on Tolman Point has its back to the sea, but this photograph illustrates how it is protected by the rocks forming the point, where no enemy could land. Any assault would have to come from inland, by troops landed in Old Town Bay, to the left, or Porth Minick, to the right.
[NMR 26580/024]

Figure 82 (left)
At Pendrathen there is the base and lower walls of a
hexagonal pillbox, cracked in two and with the roof
missing. It was a victim of coastal erosion, which has
caused it to slip from the low cliffs on the northern
shore of St Mary's on to the beach where it lies at the
Mean High Water Mark.
[DP085383]

Pendrathen, which has slid down from its cliff-top position to lie broken on the beach (Fig 82). A series of slight remains at Woolpack, close to the site of 'The Folly', in the Garrison may also be at least partly of Second World War date; low circular earthworks indicate the position of a searchlight battery and an arrangement of metal ground anchors and a cable trench suggest the presence of a guyed collapsible radio mast (Fig 83).

With peace in 1945 Scilly's long military history had apparently come to an end. However, in 1985 it was belatedly revealed that the islands could still technically be at war with the Netherlands and therefore on 17 April 1986, after 335 years of war, a 'treaty' was signed and 'peace' returned to Scilly. Today the line of the Garrison Walls is the route for a brisk walk and pillboxes serve as curiosities on hikes around St Mary's coastline. But they remain under threat; not from marauding privateers or hostile dive-bombers but from an enemy that cannot be defeated – the sea.

Figure 83 (right)
This complex of slight earthworks south-east of
Woolpack Battery incorporates remains from different
periods. The roughly square feature to the south-east
may be the footings of the building marked on historic
maps as 'The Folly' or 'Old Barracks'. Immediately to its
west are the metal pegs and footings, with a narrow
irregular trench, for a radio mast. To the north is a
circular feature partly destroyed by a later track; this,
with the other features to the west near the corner of the
Woolpack Battery, probably represents a Second World
War searchlight battery.

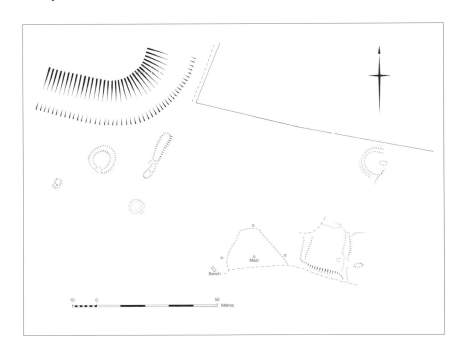

3

Scilly and the sea

At the end of the last period of glaciation, around 12,000 years ago, Scilly was probably a single large landmass. Several thousand years later, the receding ice sheet and consequent rising sea level was sufficient to separate the south-western islands of St Agnes, the Gugh and Annet from the rest of Scilly. Various authors have proposed different rates of sea-level rise, with Charles Thomas suggesting that the rest of Scilly including St Mary's, Tresco, Bryher and St Martin's only began to become distinct islands around 1,000 years ago. Subsequently other authors (Ratcliffe and Straker, and Robinson) have suggested a more gradual rise in sea levels, broadly in line with national trends. Lilly in 1715 produced a map of the islands showing that the Tresco Flats stretched to Bryher, while St Martin's Flats almost extended to Tresco. In the mid-18th century William Borlase was able to walk easily between Tresco and Bryher, a feat only possible now at the lowest of low tides.

Science has made us aware of rising sea levels, a process we now partly link to man-made climate change, but the reality is that even in the 18th and 19th century this process was under way and was observed by natural historians and visitors to Scilly. Borlase writing in 1756 had seen submerged features such as 'Hedges and Ruins' and from this observation he concluded that Tresco, Bryher and Samson were 'once one continued tract of Land, divided into Fields, and cultivated even in those low parts which are now over-run with the Sea and Sand.'[30] Aerial photographs show that on some stretches of sand flat there are the remains of submerged field boundaries, cairns, hut circles and possibly trackways, the 'Drowned Landscape' described by Charles Thomas (Fig 84). English Heritage has funded research in 2009–11, the Lyonesse project, into Scilly's submerged archaeology, using remote sensing and palaeo-environmental sampling. This will undoubtedly add colour and detail to the emerging understanding of inundation in the prehistoric period.

The causes of sea-level rise are thought to be two-fold. Over millennia, the ice that once covered much of the northern hemisphere has melted and raised the sea waters, but the creation and subsequent melting of the ice has had another impact. The thicker and longer-lasting ice sheet over Scotland pressed down the land while the thinner and newly-thawed southern parts of England rose up. Since Britain became ice-free, the reverse has been taking place, with Scotland rising from the waves while southern England sinks.

This aerial photograph shows St Agnes in the foreground, linked by a thin sandbar to the Gugh above. In the distance can be seen St Mary's with the Garrison to the fore, and in the left corner are St Martin's and the Eastern Isles.
[NMR 23896/05]

The rate is modest, but when combined with a similarly small speed of sea-level rise it contributes to an annual rate sufficient to trigger national concerns, which include the future of our coastal and low-lying heritage.

The action of the sea on the islands creates what might be described as a crenulated coastline with gently curved sections of soft geology or beaches between sharp, harder, granite headlands. When laying out batteries in the 17th century, Civil War engineers wisely chose to place batteries where the hard points occurred, interlinked with lengths of breastwork (*see* Fig 24). This arrangement probably made military sense as rocky points make direct frontal assaults more difficult, but it may also reflect an awareness of the fragility of much of the coast, a concern that is certainly reflected in documents of 18th-century date. Captain Jeffreyson in his report on the state of the

Figure 84
The wealth of underwater archaeological features is most clearly observed in aerial photographs. Submerged features on the flats beside Samson include a series of field boundaries from long-lost farmsteads.
[NMR 23941/008]

Garrison's fortifications in February 1738/9 recorded the plight of the earthwork defences along the south side of the Garrison. For instance, one note reads: '12th from Morning-point Battery to the Wool-pack Battery has been a Cover'd-Way but wants to be retired, part of the cliff being fallen into the Sea, is now uns'ble.'[31]

The stone defences of the Garrison have also suffered from the action of the sea. In 1715 Christian Lilly found a large breach at the corner of Lower Benham Battery (Fig 85) and in Jeffreyson's report he recorded that 'people at pleasure come this way into the Lines'.[32]

Rising sea level had been recognised at least by the mid-18th century and the power of the sea to cause erosion was already forcing the realignment of the Garrison's defences in the 1740s. At the same time Scilly was subjected to another feature of Britain's climate – extreme weather events. The great storm of 1744 is recorded in Robert Heath's book, published only six years later. During the afternoon of the 26 September 'the Sea rolled in vast Mountains, driven by the Winds, and broke over the Banks of *Percressa*, next the Southward, where it entered the Town with such Violence and Rapidity, as

Figure 85
Lower Benham Battery bears the marks of repeated repairs, including one resulting from a collapse in 2004. This battery at the western end of Porthcressa Beach was designed to prevent invaders getting round the end of the Garrison Walls as they existed in the late 16th century. [DP022418]

Figure 86
Hugh Town sits on a shallow sandbank between the Garrison on the right and Buzza Hill in the top left and is therefore potentially vulnerable from the sea in both directions. At the end of the quay is the Scillonian III. *[NMR 23938/20]*

threatned the levelling of all the Houses'.[33] The same storm also damaged Old Town and flooded the Lower Moors. In 1771 another large storm broke through from Porthcressa and flooded Hugh Town (Fig 86). As early as 1750 Heath suggested that the town should move to higher land and the highly judgemental Walter White writing a century later chastised the continuing development of Hugh Town:

> … on this low neck Hugh Town is built, in total disregard of consequences. The earlier settlers may have had the excuse of ignorance; but the present inhabitants, who go on building on the same spot, have a perpetual warning of what may happen in the Gugh, a small hill once similarly connected with St. Agnes. Now at high water, it is an islet. And some day, if the future may be inferred from the past, the narrow isthmus of Hugh Town will be devoured by the sea … .[34]

Between the storms of 1744 and 1771 Scilly was subjected to another major impact from the sea. Troutbeck writing in 1796 recorded that on 1 November 1755 the Isles of Scilly were hit by a tidal wave caused by an earthquake that destroyed Lisbon and killed tens of thousands of people. Like the Boxing Day earthquake in the Indian Ocean in 2004 it produced a large tsunami that reached Scilly where boats were lifted out of the sea on to the land. It is perhaps fortunate for the Garrison's defences that St Agnes would have borne the brunt of the tidal wave.

Scilly's heritage and climate change

The Isles of Scilly were created through changes to the climate; the product of millennia of ice-sheet retreat. But the rate of transformation of our environment has accelerated, particularly during the course of the 20th century, and shows no sign of decreasing in the decades ahead.

Although media controversy surrounds the global-warming debate, there is high confidence that man-made climate change is underway. While the forecasts of temperature and sea-level rises have broad ranges, there is nevertheless widespread agreement that we will have to adapt our way of life to reduce carbon emissions and to accommodate the climatic changes that are already in progress.

The fourth report of the IPCC, published in 2007, provides clear evidence of climate change during the past century. Globally, from 1906 to 2005 the world warmed by 0.74°C, though the rate of increase was faster in the past 50 years and 11 of the 12 years between 1995 and 2006 were among the warmest dozen years recorded since 1850. Global sea level has risen in line with this warming. It rose by an average of 1.8mm per year from 1961 to 2003 but at an average rate of about 3.1mm per year from 1993 to 2003.

In the 21st century it is forecast that global temperatures will rise by between 1.1°C and 6.4°C, while sea level would rise between 0.18m and 0.59m compared to the late 20th century, though this does not include the full effects of ice-sheet flow. In the most recent projections published by United Kingdom Climate Impacts Programme (UKCP09) mean summer temperatures in parts of southern England may rise by between 2.2°C and 6.8°C, while other forecasts for Scilly suggest that by 2050 sea level around the islands could rise by 0.57m. What is less easy to quantify is the rate of increase in extreme weather events, though there are reasons to expect more frequent and more severe storm events, as well as greater variation in precipitation and temperature.

Reactions to climate change in the media range from the dramatic and pessimistic to denial, and include calls for Government to respond by building huge and costly sea defences. The Department for Environment, Food and Rural Affairs (Defra) has developed a more sophisticated range of options that are reflected in Shoreline Management Plans (SMP). In these plans the coastline is divided into management units which are further divided into policy units. Projections for each policy unit are made for what could occur in the next 20, 50 and 100 years and suitable responses are suggested. The options range through advancing current defences, holding the line and managed realignment to no active intervention, where a natural, unconstrained, coastline is allowed to develop. For instance in the current SMP (SMP2) it is proposed that the stretch of St Mary's from the Quay to the Custom House will be held until after 2055 when there may be some managed realignment, while no active intervention will take place on uninhabited stretches of the coast.

The impact of climate change will be most acutely felt in the low-lying parts of Scilly, particularly Hugh Town (Fig 87). Parts of Old Town and the Lower Moors to the west of the town may be prone to inundation. Scilly could also be affected by an increase in extreme weather events, with locations around the edges of the islands that do not face on to The Road being particularly vulnerable to major storms. However, some of the worst effects of this can be mitigated by good maintenance of buildings and by using appropriate high-quality materials. Advice on how to carry out robust repairs that are sympathetic to the historic environment can be provided by the Conservation Officer and the Planning Department of the Council of the Isles of Scilly and English Heritage.

Figure 87
This view of the Town Beach at Hugh Town at a serene high tide shows how close the sea already comes to buildings along the shore. Even small rises in sea level will make flooding a more frequent event. [DP085180]

The most immediate effect on Scilly's heritage may not come from any of these factors, but from coastal erosion. An article published jointly by specialist staff from English Heritage, the National Trust and the Environment Agency succinctly summed up the issue:

Coasts are dynamic, but historic assets are fixed.[35]

Coastal erosion is already obvious on St Mary's. The path along the east side of Porthcressa has been diverted inland recently and at Tolman Point the road edge is crumbling away. Descending on to the rocks around the island, erosion is seen to be more widespread. At a number of locations large caverns have been carved into the soft geology of low cliffs where only the overhanging mat of vegetation is holding the undercut topsoil together. After a number of years this arrangement can no longer continue and some or all of the overhanging soil collapses on to the shore. Such partial falls can be seen near Woolpack where a roughly 4m wide and 3m deep cavern has recently partially collapsed and similar falls can be seen at Halangy Point (Figs 88 and 89). Forecasts of erosion on St Mary's over the next hundred years suggest that much of Scilly's coastal heritage is at risk, but conversely coastal erosion is also revealing new archaeological finds. For instance, at Halangy Porth erosion is revealing prehistoric artefacts as the soft coastline crumbles and the Isles of Scilly Museum has a growing collection of material coming from this type of source, though these artefacts may lack a specific, archaeological context. For larger features at such sites, such as the stone structures and middens at Halangy Porth, there is a need to monitor, record and manage the larger elements that cannot be relocated to the museum.

Defra has recognised that the coast can only be defended where it is sustainable and affordable. Priorities for investment have to be identified and at least initially funding will be concentrated on large coastal settlements. For instance, a major scheme of sea defences is underway at Blackpool where a sophisticated programme is advancing the defences to dissipate wave energy without having to raise the height of the sea defences. Portsmouth's future is being considered at present, as if no action is taken parts of the town could disappear, and the home base of the Royal Navy could be compromised. On other less-populated parts of the coast modest

Figure 88
The largest example of undercut coastline lies just to the east of King Charles' Battery where a 6m wide and 4m deep hole has been eroded to within a few metres of the nearby stretch of the Garrison Walls.
[DP086073]

Figure 89
The pace of the erosion at the south end of the Garrison was accelerated by the remains of a shipping container from the Cita on the shore that replicated the effect of an industrial grinder with a large chunk of metal being repeatedly driven by the waves on to the soft, low cliff. The wreckage has now been cleared.
[DP022631]

short-term provision for sea defences may be provided, but for most of the coastline some limited reshaping of the natural landscape combined with letting the sea find its new, natural level will be the normal response.

Even if we could afford to protect all of the coast this would have a highly deleterious effect on the natural and historic environment of the coast. Following the catastrophic floods of January 1953 on the Essex coast a high wall was built to protect Jaywick Sands from the sea. Now, in place of a sea view, the bungalow dwellers face a concrete wall, which must be climbed to reach the beach.

Change is inevitable; what matters is how this change is managed. Priorities will need to be identified by partnerships made up of communities, local and national government and the appropriate natural and historic agencies that have vested interests in securing a future for our coast. Inevitably the first priority will be to secure people's homes, jobs and the infrastructure of settlements, and there is a danger that the historical remains of our island nation may be neglected.

English Heritage recognises that there are no circumstances in which all this precious heritage can be protected, but this does not mean that much cannot be achieved, even with the limited resources available. The normal response will be to monitor the threat and to intervene where appropriate. In exceptional circumstances an historic structure can be relocated, the most famous examples perhaps being the Egyptian monuments moved to survive the creation of the Aswan Dam. Relocations have taken place in Britain; for instance Clavell Tower overlooking Kimmeridge Bay in Dorset was moved 25m inland by the Landmark Trust and consideration is being given to moving the 1844 Trinity House Landmark at Portland Bill.

Relocation will only ever be an exceptional response, one that is unlikely to be appropriate in Scilly, and providing new, hard defences to protect coastal heritage will only be appropriate where it proves to be sustainable and affordable, and will not cause greater damage further along the coast (Fig 90). The standard, and perhaps the most appropriate, reaction to the threat to coastal heritage will be to record it so that if it is lost a suitable record will survive for posterity. Recording should be seen as a positive response rather than a negative, almost defeatist reaction. Some endangered sites will feature within English Heritage's *Heritage at Risk* initiative and a research

Figure 90
At King Charles' Battery at the north of the Garrison a previous cavern undermining the cliff has been reinforced by concrete sandbags to prevent its collapse.
[DP086023]

framework for Scilly is being developed and coastal features at risk will be central to this strategy.

All recording consists of three distinct phases. Firstly there is the need to identify the historical assets of a defined area and this can be done through the use of maps, documentary sources, aerial photography, fieldwork and by drawing on local knowledge. The conservation grazing programme undertaken by the Isles of Scilly Wildlife Trust has revealed new military sites of interest, such as a Second World War command or machine gun post near

Figure 91 (left)
On the hillside near Innisidgen the aerial photograph shows clearly a V-shaped battery with flanking breastwork and another horizontal structure along the front of it. On the ground the same site is still covered with neck-high vegetation and cannot be investigated or recorded until the site is cleared. [NMR 26579/20]

Figure 92 (right)
This drawing was created from a rectified photograph and therefore is an accurate scale drawing. It shows clearly that the Garrison Gate has been inserted into the earlier fabric of the defences shown at the bottom left corner of the drawing.

Bant's Carn and it has also revealed sites that were known, but had not been seen for a generation (Fig 91).

Once identified there are two further inter-connected stages, involving the processes of understanding and documenting historic assets. This publication offers an appreciation of the development of Scilly's military heritage and more of the detailed documentary research that lies behind this book will be published in the form of complimentary articles in local and national journals. As part of the project more than one thousand high-quality photographs, including aerial photography, have been created and deposited in the National Monuments Record. To supplement this, selective rectified photography and photogrammetry has taken place on part of the Garrison Walls (Fig 92). This research project as a whole has gathered and created extensive archives, but there still remains much to do to establish a comprehensive record of Scilly's military history before much of it succumbs to the power of the sea.

Conclusion

The sea is the insatiable monster, which devours these little islands, gorges itself with the earth, sand, clay, and all the yielding parts, and leaves nothing, where it can reach, but the skeleton, the bared rock. The continual advances, which the sea makes upon the low-lands, at present, are plain to all people of observation, and within these last thirty years have been very considerable.[36]

Borlase writing in the 1750s vividly described the power of the sea, and he recognised that there was nothing that could be done to stem it. Today strategies have begun to be put in place to address the growing threat from rising sea levels, increasingly turbulent weather patterns and the consequent increased rate of coastal erosion. Relocation of monuments and the construction of hard defences will be an occasional response in Britain, but the reality is that change and loss have to be accepted and managed. Recording will play a key part in any strategies dealing with coastal heritage and underpinning this must be a thorough appreciation of the history of endangered sites.

Scilly is a destination for lovers of flowers, for bird watchers in search of rare feathered visitors blown on to the islands by Atlantic winds, and for people in search of serene, natural beauty. However, it also boasts an unrivalled military heritage, acquired as each successive threat to Britain was met by new defences. Until the 20th century, the absence of significant pressure for development meant that many of these accumulated layers of our military past have survived for successive generations to discover, study and enjoy. No other settlement of this modest size can boast such a rich military heritage. Hopefully, in the future the Isles of Scilly may become a place of pilgrimage for people in search of the story of Britain's colourful military history. As well as gannets, the gunners of Scilly deserve celebration.

This view from the Old Blockhouse on Tresco shows the area that was at the heart of the Parliamentarian assault on Tresco in April 1651. [DP085142]

Notes

1 Borlase 1966, 33

2 Calendar of State Papers Domestic 14 March 1602

3 Toulmin Smith 1964, 190; Borlase 1966, 8

4 Acts of the Privy Council of England Volume II 1547–30 London: HMSO 1890, 354; Calendar of State Papers Domestic 5 November 1549

5 Acts of the Privy Council of England 28 May 1627, 301

6 Acts of the Privy Council of England 27 May 1551, 282

7 Hatfield House Drawing reference CPM II, 34

8 Acts of the Privy Council of England 30 September 1551, 373

9 Acts of the Privy Council of England 20 March 1591

10 Calendar of State Papers Domestic August 1593

11 Calendar of State Papers Domestic April 1600

12 Calendar of State Papers Domestic 3 April 1627; Acts of the Privy Council 28 May 1627

13 Calendar of State Papers Domestic 30 September 1637

14 Pounds 1984, 137; Lilly 1715, 5v

15 Lilly 1715, 5r

16 National Archives WO51/124, 11v

17 National Archives WO55/350, 45

18 National Archives WO55/350, 44–5

19 National Archives WO51/144, 105

20 National Archives WO51/157, 123; WO51/161, 132

21 National Archives WO51/156, 218

22 National Archives WO51/161, 132

23 Borlase 1966, 10

24 Troutbeck 1796, 41

25 White 1855, 260

26 National Archives WO78/4100

27 National Archives CAB/65/8/50

28 National Archives CAB/66/11/30

29 Isles of Scilly Museum, 'Scillonian War Diary 1939–45' vol iii, Appendix aE, 36

30 Borlase 1966, 26

31 National Archives WO55/350, 45

32 Lilly 1715 5v, 6r; National Archives WO55/350, 45

33 Heath 1967, 28

34 White 1855, 249

35 Murphy 2009, 9

36 Borlase 1753–4, 57

References and further reading

Abbatiello, J J 2006 *Anti-Submarine Warfare in World War One: British naval aviation and the defeat of the U-boats*. London: Routledge

Adams, F and P 1984 *Star Castle and its Garrison*. St Mary's: Belvedere Press Ltd and Francis and Pam Adams

Barratt, J 2006 *Cromwell's Wars at Sea*. Barnsley: Pen & Sword Military

Borlase, W 1753–4 'An Account of the Great Alterations which the Islands of Sylley have Undergone since the Time of the Antients, … '. *Philosophical Transactions of the Royal Society of London* **48**, 55–69

Borlase, W 1966 *Observations on the Islands of Scilly*. Newcastle-upon-Tyne: Frank Graham (originally published in 1756)

Cassar, M 2005 *Climate Change and the Historic Environment*. London: Centre for Sustainable Heritage, University College London. *See* http://www.ucl.ac.uk/sustainableheritage/climate_change.htm (accessed 8 December 2010)

Clarke, G S 1989 *Fortification*, 2 edn. Liphook: Beaufort (originally published in 1890)

Colvin, H M (ed) 1982 *The History of the King's Works*, Vol IV: 1485–1660. London: HMSO

Defra 2010 *Adapting to Coastal Change: Developing a Policy Framework*
See http://www.defra.gov.uk/environment/flooding/manage/coastalchange.htm (accessed 8 December 2010)

English Heritage 2008 *Climate Change and the Historic Environment*
See http://www.english-heritage.org.uk/publications/climate-change-and-the-historic-environment/ (accessed 8 December 2010)

Fulford, M, Champion, T and Long, A 1997 *England's Coastal Heritage*. London: RCHME and English Heritage

Goodwin, J 1993 'Granite Towers on St Mary's, Isles of Scilly' *Cornish Archaeology* **32**, 128–39

Heath, R 1967 *A Natural and Historical Account of the Islands of Scilly*. Newcastle-upon-Tyne: Frank Graham (originally published in 1750)

Intergovernmental Panel on Climate Change
See http://www.ipcc.ch/ (accessed 8 December 2010)

Johns, C, Larn, R and Perry Tapper, B 2004 *Rapid Coastal Zone Assessment for the Isles of Scilly*. Truro: Historic Environmental Service, Cornwall County Council
See http://www.english-heritage.org.uk/publications/isles-of-scilly-rczas/ (accessed 8 December 2010)

Lilly, C 1715 *Survey of the Fortifications in Plymouth Division by Col Christian Lily 1714–1717*. London: British Library King's Manuscript 45

London, P 1999 *U-Boat Hunters: Cornwall's air war 1916–1919*. Truro: Dyllansow Truran

Longmate, N 1993 Island Fortress: *The defence of Great Britain 1603–1945*. London: Grafton

Longmate, N 2001 *Defending the Island*. London: Pimlico

Maurice-Jones, K W 2005 *The History of Coast Artillery in the British Army*. Uckfield: Naval and Military Press in association with Firepower, the Royal Artillery Museum

Miles, T J and Saunders, A D 1970 'King Charles' Castle, Tresco, Scilly'. *Post Medieval Archaeology* **4**, 1–30

Murphy, P, Thackray, D and Wilson, E 2009 'Coastal Heritage and Climate Change in England: Assessing Threats and Priorities'. *Conservation and Management of Archaeological Sites*, **11:1**, 9–15

Murphy, P 2009 *The English Coast*. London: Continuum

Osborne, J P 'Scillonian War Diary 1914–1918'. Unpublished, Isles of Scilly Museum

Osborne, J P 'Scillonian War Diary 1939–1945'. Unpublished, Isles of Scilly Museum

Porter, W 1951 *History of the Corps of Royal Engineers*. Chatham: The Institution of Royal Engineers (two volumes; originally published in 1889)

Pounds, N J (ed) 1984 *The Parliamentary Survey of the Duchy of Cornwall*, Pt 2. Exeter: Devon and Cornwall Record Society

Powell, J R 1931 'Blake's Reduction of the Scilly Isles in 1651'. *Mariners Mirror* **17:3**, 205–22

Putley, J 2003 *The Isles of Scilly in the English Civil Wars*. Bristol: Stuart Press

Quinnell, N V 1978 'A 16th Century Outwork to King Charles' Castle, Tresco'. *Cornish Archaeology* 17, 142–3

Ratcliffe, J and Straker, V 1996 *The Early Environment of Scilly*. Cornwall: Cornwall Archaeological Unit

Robinson, G 2007 *The Prehistoric Island Landscapes of Scilly*. BAR British Series 447. Oxford: Archaeopress

Saunders, A D 1962 'Harry's Walls, St Mary's, Scilly: A new interpretation'. *Cornish Archaeology* **I**, 85–91

Saunders, A D 1989 *Fortress Britain*. Liphook: Beaufort

Sherburne, E 1661 *Survey of Stores and Arms with Statement of Repairs Needed (Plymouth and Western Garrisons)*. National Archives WO55/1697

Shoreline Management Plan 2
See http://www.ciscag.org (accessed 8 December 2010)

Toulmin Smith, L (ed) 1964 *The Itinerary of John Leland*, Vol 1. London: Centaur Press

Thomas, C 1985 *Exploration of a Drowned Landscape*. London: BT Batsford

Troutbeck, J 1796 *A Survey of the Ancient and Present State of the Scilly Isles*. Sherborne: Goadby and Lerpiniere

United Kingdom Climate Impacts Programme (UKCP09)
See http://ukclimateprojections.defra.gov.uk/ (accessed 8 December 2010)

White, W 1855 *A Londoner's Walk to Land's End: And a trip to the Scilly Isles*. London: Chapman and Hall

Woodley, G 1822 *A View of the Present State of the Scilly Islands*. London

Other titles in the Informed Conservation series

Behind the Veneer: The South Shoreditch furniture trade and its buildings.
Joanna Smith and Ray Rogers, 2006. ISBN 9781873592960

Berwick-upon-Tweed: Three places, two nations, one town.
Adam Menuge with Cathcrinc Dcwar, 2009.
ISBN 9781848020290

The Birmingham Jewellery Quarter: An introduction and guide.
John Cattell and Bob Hawkins, 2000. ISBN 9781850747772

Bridport and West Bay: The buildings of the flax and hemp industry.
Mike Williams, 2006. ISBN 9781873592861

Building a Better Society: Liverpool's historic institutional buildings.
Colum Giles, 2008. ISBN 9781873592908

Built on Commerce: Liverpool's central business district.
Joseph Sharples and John Stonard, 2008. ISBN 9781905624348

Built to Last? The buildings of the Northamptonshire boot and shoe industry.
Kathryn A Morrison with Ann Bond, 2004. ISBN 9781873592793

England's Schools: History, architecture and adaptation.
Elain Harwood, 2010. ISBN 9781848020313

English Garden Cities: An introduction.
Mervyn Miller, 2010. ISBN 9781848020511

Gateshead: Architecture in a changing English urban landscape.
Simon Taylor and David Lovie, 2004. ISBN 9781873592762

Manchester's Northern Quarter.
Simon Taylor and Julian Holder, 2008. ISBN 9781873592847

Manchester: The warehouse legacy – An introduction and guide.
Simon Taylor, Malcolm Cooper and P S Barnwell, 2002.
ISBN 9781873592670

Manningham: Character and diversity in a Bradford suburb.
Simon Taylor and Kathryn Gibson, 2010. ISBN 9781848020306

Margate's Seaside Heritage.
Nigel Barker, Allan Brodie, Nick Dermott, Lucy Jessop and Gary Winter, 2007. ISBN 9781905624669

Newcastle's Grainger Town: An urban renaissance.
Fiona Cullen and David Lovie, 2003. ISBN 9781873592779

'One Great Workshop': The buildings of the Sheffield metal trades.
Nicola Wray, Bob Hawkins and Colum Giles, 2001.
ISBN 9781873592663

Ordinary Landscapes, Special Places: Anfield, Breckfield and the growth of Liverpool's suburbs.
Adam Menuge, 2008. ISBN 9781873592892

Places of Health and Amusement: Liverpool's historic parks and gardens.
Katy Layton-Jones and Robert Lee, 2008. ISBN 9781873592915

Plymouth: Vision of a modern city.
Jeremy Gould, 2010. ISBN 9781848020504

Religion and Place in Leeds.
John Minnis with Trevor Mitchell, 2007. ISBN 9781905624485

Religion and Place: Liverpool's historic places of worship.
Sarah Brown and Peter de Figueiredo, 2008. ISBN 9781873592885

Stourport-on-Severn: Pioneer town of the canal age.
Colum Giles, Keith Falconer, Barry Jones and Michael Taylor, 2007.
ISBN 9781905624362

Weymouth's Seaside Heritage.
Allan Brodie, Colin Ellis, David Stuart and Gary Wintcr, 2008.
ISBN 9781848020085

Further information on titles in the Informed Conservation series can be found on our website.

To order through EH Sales
Tel: 0845 458 9910
Fax: 0845 458 9912
Email: eh@centralbooks.com
Online bookshop: www.english-heritageshop.org.uk

Gazetteer of principal sites of interest

Map 1 – Isles of Scilly

❶ Tresco, King Charles' Castle (*see* p 1 and Figs 6, 7, 8, 9 and 10)
King Charles' Castle is a small, stone fort of the late 1540s overlooking New Grimsby Harbour from high up on Castle Down. It has a polygonal gun platform and attached domestic accommodation. Earthwork fortifications, probably of early 17th-century date, cover the northern side.

❷ Tresco, earthwork on Castle Down (*see* Fig 11)
This long, shallow earthwork, probably of the 1550s, incorporates angled bastions. It seems to have been designed to protect against advances up from New Grimsby but was never completed.

❸ Tresco, Cromwell's Castle (*see* p 1 and Figs 33, 34, 35 and 36)
Cromwell's Castle consists of a tall stone tower of the early 1650s with an attached gun platform, perhaps rebuilt during the 18th century. The inside walls are marked with excellent graffiti, some possibly carved by gunners during the 18th century.

❹ Tresco, the Old Blockhouse (*see* Figs 3, 4, 5 and p 89)
This small stone fortification of the late 1540s consists of a single heated room for domestic accommodation beside a small gun platform that may have had three guns. It is surrounded by a slight earthwork.

❺ Tresco, site of seaplane base (*see* Figs 71, 72 and 73)
A seaplane base operated in New Grimsby Harbour from 1917 until the end of the First World War. The site is now largely occupied by modern holiday accommodation.

❻ Tresco, Oliver's Battery (*see* Fig 32)
This battery was begun at the end of April 1651 to house guns to bombard ships in St Mary's Harbour. It is set to the south of the large outcrop of rock, a short distance from the Carn Near jetty.

❼ St Martin's, signal station (*see* Fig 60)
Built in 1804 beside the day mark and abandoned a decade later, the signal station consists of a small domestic structure with ancillary buildings set within two compounds.

❽ The Gugh, Carn of Works Civil War battery
This earthwork battery in the gulls' nesting area has two bastion-like gun positions to the front and a narrow entrance at the rear.

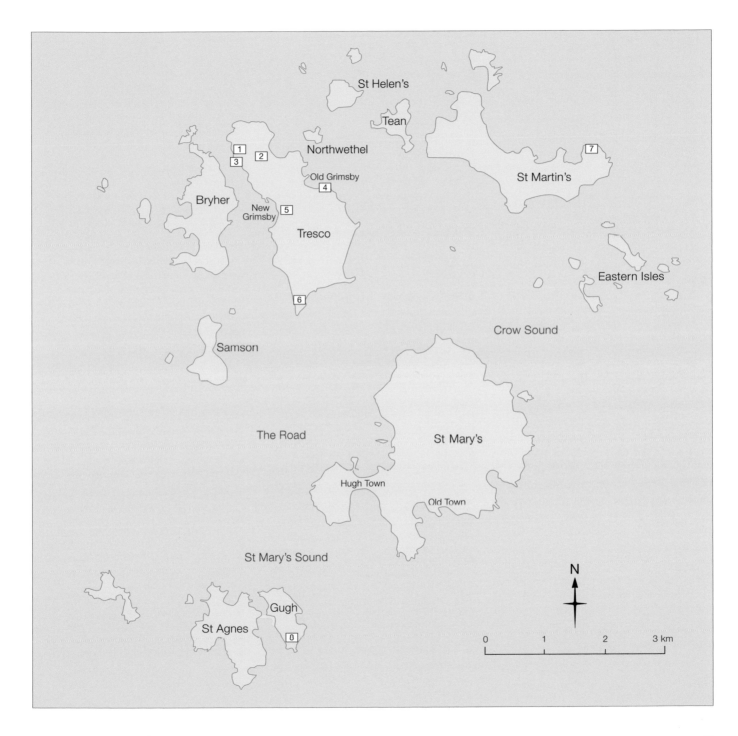

St Helen's

Tean

Northwethel

1
2
3

Old Grimsby
4

Bryher

New
Grimsby
5

St Martin's
7

Tresco

6

Eastern Isles

Samson

Crow Sound

The Road

St Mary's

Hugh Town

Old Town

St Mary's Sound

Gugh

St Agnes

0

N

0   1   2   3 km

Map 2 – St Mary's

❾ Site of seaplane base at Porthmellon
In 1917 there was a short-lived attempt to create a naval seaplane base on the shore but the bay proved unsuitable for the purpose.

❿ Harry's Walls (*see* front cover, p 4 and Figs 12, 13 and 14)
Begun in 1551 and never completed, its design proves that it was one of the most sophisticated military structures of its period.

⓫ Pillbox at Newford Island
Set on the shore beside Newford Island this well-hidden pillbox is part of the chain built in 1941.

⓬ Morval Point Civil War battery and bivouac platform (*see* Figs 24 and 25)
One of the best-preserved Civil War batteries, a V-shaped earthwork, it is located on the cliff near a golf tee; the square platform to the north is probably of later date.

⓭ Telegraph Tower (*see* Fig 59)
Built in 1814 and closed in 1816, this imposing tower was an Admiralty signal station. It was later used by the coastguards.

⓮ Bant's Carn quick- firing battery
Built at the beginning of the 20th century, this battery's guns were never installed due to a change in the geo-politics of Europe.

⓯ Pillbox at Pendrathen (*see* Fig 82)
Due to coastal erosion, the pillbox has fallen off the shallow cliff and now lies on the beach.

⓰ Civil War battery and platforms above Little Porth
Set within thick undergrowth are the remains of Civil War earthworks and possibly accompanying bivouac platforms.

⓱ Breastwork and batteries at Innisidgen and Block House Point (*see* Fig 91)
Along the edge of the coastal path some stretches of Civil War breastwork have survived, along with traces of earthwork batteries.

⓲ Battery on Helvear Hill (*see* Fig 27)
This site was cleared of vegetation in 2008 revealing a large, earthwork gun battery on the hilltop.

⓳ Remains of the Old Blockhouse at Block House Point
On the shore, this very overgrown rectangular structure may be a blockhouse of the 16th century. It was used by shipping as a navigation aid until the 18th century.

⓴ Batteries at Trenear's Rock
Set into the hillside there is at least one battery, revealed in 2010 when thick undergrowth was cleared.

㉑ Pellew's Redoubt (*see* Fig 26)
On Toll's Island this small battery, similar to the one on the Gugh, and associated breastworks probably date from the Civil War.

㉒ Mount Todden (*see* Figs 28, 29, 30 and 76)
This large earthwork encloses a watchhouse or signal station that could be an adaptation of a chambered cairn. Beside it are the remains of structures for a Second World War aircraft blind-flying beacon.

㉓ Normandy Down, arrow (*see* Fig 77)
A large concrete arrow, flush with the ground, is probably a range marker in connection with the Crow Sound floating target. There is also a small, ruinous, polygonal concrete structure of military origin beside it, probably part of the post-Second World War Rotor VHF installation.

㉔ Memorial to Sir Cloudesley Shovell
Sir Cloudesley Shovell was a highly successful Admiral of the Fleet fighting in Spanish waters, but on his return to England in 1707 his ship and others ran aground on Scilly's Western Rocks.

㉕ Pillbox at Porth Hellick
Overlooking the bay and Shovell's monument there is a small, Second World War pillbox set on the low cliff.

㉖ Giant's Castle
Despite being a 'castle' in name, this prehistoric structure was originally probably ceremonial in function. During the Second World War a rifle range and air gunnery range was established beside it.

㉗ Civil War earthwork battery near end of airport runway
This battery on Church Point consists of shallow earthworks, now damaged, and perhaps a nearby bivouac platform.

㉘ Pillbox at Tolman Point (*see* Fig 80 and 81)
On Tolman Point this fairly standard pillbox seems to face the wrong way with its door facing out to sea rather than inland, but tactically its orientation is correct as an enemy could only land in one of the bays to either side, not on the rocks behind.

㉙ Cat's Coffin pillbox in Old Town (*see* Fig 78)
On the road through Old Town, this pillbox is set into the front wall of the garden of a modern house and is very easy to miss.

㉚ Pillbox on path towards the Old Church
Like the Cat's Coffin, this pillbox on the path to the church was built to protect Old Town Bay.

㉛ Civil War earthwork battery at Carn Leh
Slight remains of a Civil War battery seem to survive under dense vegetation.

㉜ Earthwork battery at Peninnis Head
A battery that may date from the early 18th century with what may be an attached bivouac platform survives here. However, this battery is very poorly placed for firing out to sea.

㉝ Buzza Hill Tower
Once thought to be one of Major Lyman's gun towers, it is apparently the last windmill to have been built in Scilly.

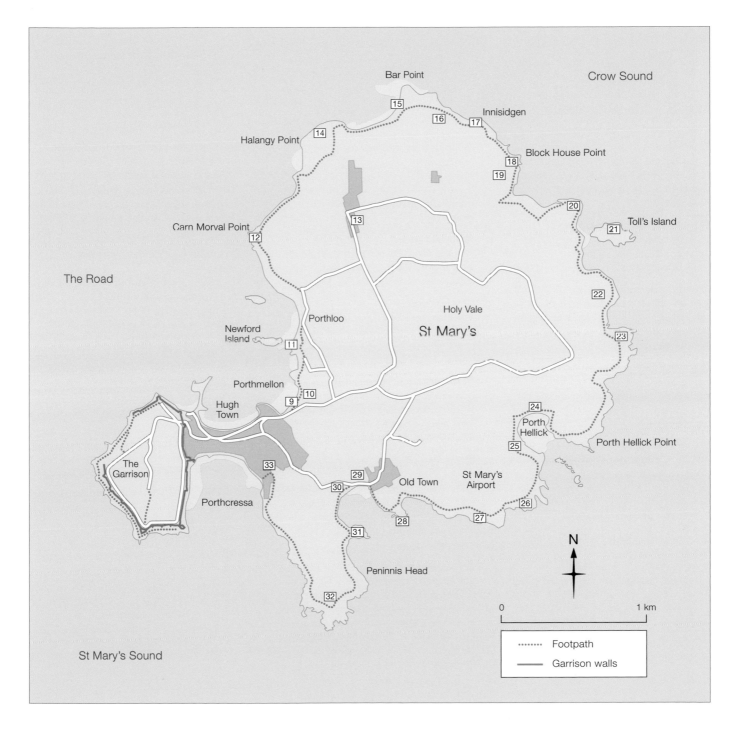

Bar Point

Crow Sound

15

Innisidgen

16   17

Halangy Point

14

Block House Point

18

19

Carn Morval Point

13

20

Toll's Island

12

21

The Road

22

Holy Vale

23

Porthloo

St Mary's

Newford
Island

11

Porthmellon

10

9

Hugh
Town

24

Porth
Hellick

Porth Hellick Point

25

33

Porthcressa

The
Garrison

29

Old Town

St Mary's
Airport

26

30

28

27

31

Peninnis Head

32

N

0   1 km

.... Footpath

——— Garrison walls

St Mary's Sound

Map 3 – The Garrison on St Mary's

㉞ Storehouse
Beside Newman's Platform, this storehouse was designed by Christian Lilly in 1715 and plans for it appear in his manuscript in the British Library.

㉟ Former Master Gunner's house
Lilly also suggested providing the Master Gunner, the formidable Abraham Tovey, with his own house. This is now the White House.

㊱ Star Castle (*see* Figs 15, 16, 17, 18 and 37)
Built in 1593–4, the castle remained the base for the Governor and the centre of military command in Scilly until the Second World War. It is now a luxury hotel.

㊲ Powder magazine (*see* Figs 20 and 21)
Probably built in the 1620s but with significant strengthening of its walls in the 18th century, this magazine is set within a compound tucked into the hillside.

㊳ Garrison Gate (*see* Figs 19, 39 and 92)
Bearing Abraham Tovey's initials and the date 1742, this replaced an earlier gate which was flanked by two 17th-century buildings that were used as barracks. These are now domestic accommodation.

㊴ Defence Electric Light Position and pillbox
At the beginning of the 20th century a searchlight position was constructed at Steval Point but never activated. During the Second World War a small pillbox was created just above it.

㊵ Steval Point quick-firing battery
(*see* Fig 70)
This is one of the two quick-firing batteries of the early 20th century. The accompanying small barracks building is now a private house.

㊶ Steval battery
This was one of the two large gun batteries built in 1898–1901. It is now used by the gun club.

㊷ Signal tower
This tower became a signal station during the 19th century but it was originally one of a pair of older windmills. It was never used as a gun tower.

㊸ Barracks (*see* Figs 61 and 66)
Between Woolpack and Steval batteries a large barracks block was built set within its own, separate earthwork. It is now used as holiday accommodation.

㊹ Woolpack Battery (*see* Figs 61, 62, 63, 64, 65 and 75)
The second gun battery of 1898–1901, reused for a 'RACON' beacon during the Second World War, now provides accommodation for volunteers working for the Isles of Scilly Wildlife Trust.

㊺ Possible remains of the Folly and 20th-century features (*see* Fig 83)
Set on the hillside beneath Woolpack are earthworks of probably Second World War origin and a square structure that may be the remains of the Folly, possibly a medieval or 16th-century structure later used as a barracks.

㊻ Defence Electric Light Control Point
(*see* Fig 69)
The two searchlights at Steval Point and in front of Woolpack were used along with this small control centre set into the hillside above the 18th-century Woolpack Battery to locate enemy shipping.

㊼ Defence Electric Light Position
(*see* Fig 68)
The small concrete structure in front of the 18th-century Woolpack Battery is a searchlight position of the early 20th century, designed to illuminate ships for the guns to target from the hills above.